# PRAISE FOR *WINNING HER BUSINESS*

"Bridget Brennan provides us with a wonderful guide to navigating the world of women consumers. In *Winning Her Business*, Brennan gives readers valuable insights that can be leveraged from the corner office to the sales floor."

—INDRA K. NOOYI, Chairman, PepsiCo

"In an era of unmatched speed, convenience, selection, and price, winning her business requires mastering every element of the customer experience, including human interaction. Brennan's Four Motivators Framework® is a smart and scalable road map to actionable changes that every business can leverage to succeed with one of the world's largest growth markets."

—TOM BARTLEY, Head of Retail, Google

"At a time when a great customer experience is the expectation, Bridget Brennan's book is right on target. Her research and insight offer a practical guide to providing a tailored customer experience for the largest growth market—women! Her logical approach is intuitive and actionable for both men and women alike. This book should be required reading for all leaders, in order for their business to succeed in a modern economy."

—PEGGY TURNER, Vice President, Guest Retention and Satisfaction, Lexus

"Bridget Brennan is opening up our eyes to a compelling reality and to a significant business opportunity. Brennan's new book is visionary and at the same time pragmatic and practical. It is a must read for anyone interested in enhancing the customer experience and looking for new business opportunities."

—LAURENT FREIXE, Executive Vice President and CEO, Zone Americas, Nestlé S.A.

"*Winning Her Business* is a powerful resource for any business leader who aspires to create inclusive customer experiences, stay relevant, and forge authentic bonds with America's new consumer. The book is chock full of highly actionable insights, and Brennan's Four Motivators Framework® should be leverageable for any business, regardless of industry, across all dimensions of difference, including gender and beyond."

—SANDY CROSS, Senior Director of Diversity and Inclusion, PGA of America

"Few know more about female customers than Bridget Brennan. In *Winning Her Business* she shows how to transform the customer experience for women by engaging their whole selves. If you want to tap into an increasingly powerful customer base, this is the book for you."

—FLORIAN ZETTELMEYER, Nancy L. Ertle Professor of Marketing, Chair, Marketing Department, Kellogg School of Management, Northwestern University

"An insightful perspective on how women drive consumption and how they see buying. The book is an easy-to-read, practical guide for modern sales and customer service leaders, and it is relevant to many categories and contexts. Considering the female perspective is a global business issue, accelerated in the digital age and relevant across all the world."

—FABIO VACIRCA, Senior Managing Director – Products, Africa, Middle East, Asia-Pacific, Accenture

"If your business is aiming to win with women, then this is the book for you. Bridget Brennan doesn't just provide powerful ideas on how to connect with women, but also the directive to put insight into action for meaningful impact on your business."

—INGA STENTA, Head of Global Business Growth, Reebok

"Women have been instrumental to the growth of the snowboarding business and lifestyle. Brennan shows us that winning is all about inclusivity. Spend an hour with this book, and watch your customer communication skills grow."

—ELYSA WALK, Senior Vice President and General Manager, Americas, Burton Snowboards

"Brennan connects with the reader in the precise way she recommends we reach the female customer: with inspiration, confidence, and appreciation of your time."

"Bridget Brennan's point is clear: focusing on the female consumer will have deep, economic benefit. Her tactics and best practices for knowing and understanding the customer are crucial for anyone seeking to grow their business."

# WINNING HER BUSINESS

## HOW TO TRANSFORM THE CUSTOMER EXPERIENCE FOR THE WORLD'S MOST POWERFUL CONSUMERS

## BRIDGET BRENNAN

HarperCollins
Leadership

An Imprint of HarperCollins

Published by HarperCollins Leadership, an imprint of HarperCollins Focus LLC.

Any internet addresses, phone numbers, or company or product information printed in this book are offered as a resource and are not intended in any way to be or to imply an endorsement by HarperCollins Leadership, nor does HarperCollins Leadership vouch for the existence, content, or services of these sites, phone numbers, companies, or products beyond the life of this book.

Unless otherwise noted, quotations in this book were taken from personal interviews with business owners, executives. customers, and sales professionals.

The Four Motivators® Framework is a registered trademark of Female Factor Corp. All rights reserved.

ISBN 978-1-4002-0998-9 (eBook)
ISBN 978-1-4002-0997-2 (HC)
ISBN 978-1-4002-1000-8 (TP)
ISBN 978-1-4002-1293-4 (IE)

**Library of Congress Cataloging-in-Publication Data**
Library of Congress Control Number: 2018959503

*Printed in the United States of America*
19 20 21 22 23  LSC  10 9 8 7 6 5 4 3 2 1

*To Erik, for everything*

# CONTENTS

# CONTENTS

# INTRODUCTION

It was a cold, rainy day as I walked down the boardwalk in Atlantic City, New Jersey, taking a break from a conference I was attending nearby. I looked at the string of empty stores and felt sorry for the shop owners, wondering how they made a living in this decaying retail district.

Imagine my surprise when I walked into one of the stores, looking for a souvenir to bring home, and was ignored by the lone employee who stood just a few feet away, leaning against the counter and staring into his phone. Since I was the only other person in the store, I thought he'd be thrilled to have a customer. I was wrong. He didn't even look up.

The minutes ticked by, and I started to wonder, *How long will it take for this guy to acknowledge me?* The store was so small that our silent impasse felt awkward. After several minutes, I gave up and left the store empty-handed and irritated. In my head I was shouting, *Hey, I was doing you a favor just by coming here!* Then I walked back to the conference I was attending and took the stage to deliver a presentation I'd been hired to give. The topic? How to create great customer experiences.

The timing was ironic, but my experience in the store wasn't shocking. Bad service is everywhere, at every price point, in every industry. And yet, many businesses still don't seem to recognize the link between the quality of service they give and their customers' buying decisions. They search and search for the newest idea for winning business and end up overlooking the most obvious strategy of all: create an experience so satisfying that people will want to spend their time and money with the company, and refer it to everyone they know.

Common sense? Yes. Common practice? No. Just ask any woman.

Women are on the receiving end of most customer experiences, good and bad, because they control the majority of the world's consumer spending. It's estimated they drive upward of 70 to 80 percent of consumer spending in the United States alone through a combination of buying power and influence.[1] Earning their business is the key to winning in the modern economy. Yet most sales training programs overlook the simple question of whether the buyer is a man or a woman. This is both a blind spot and an opportunity: a blind spot because outdated stereotypes about women are pervasive and can stop a sale in its tracks, and an opportunity because understanding women's perspectives is a serious competitive advantage for anyone in sales.

Men and women can view sales interactions through different lenses. As a researcher on women's buying decisions, I routinely hear stories about poor sales experiences that drive women away from buying products and services. Many women report being

- treated with less respect simply because of their gender,
- judged on their appearance in ways that men are not, and
- ignored, overlooked, or underestimated when shopping with a male partner or companion.

The last one is a frequent issue. Countless women have told me about not receiving eye contact or attention when shopping with a male partner, even when a salesperson was told that the product was for her. Casual sexism is commonplace ("Tell your husband he should buy this necklace for you."), and so is unconscious bias and stereotyping ("I'm surprised a woman wants a stick shift. Are you sure?"). In customer interactions, all kinds of things happen to women that would be inconceivable if they were men. Consider the experience of a customer we'll call Rachel, a woman in her late twenties whose loyalty to a major hotel brand was tested by an unfortunate experience during a business trip.

"My (older, male) boss and I got in line separately to check in at a hotel in Miami," Rachel begins. "This was a big hotel, part of a well-known chain. While we were standing there, the hotel associate looked over at me, then back at my boss, and said, 'I don't have your rooms available yet, but I do have one available for an hour,' and winked. I was new at my job and mortified that someone had assumed I was my boss's escort."

Rachel's story isn't from some bygone era: it happened today, to a highly educated, well-paid executive with an active social media presence (in other words, a megaphone), who can afford to take her business—and loyalty—elsewhere.

The business-to-business (B2B) world is no different. I've heard many stories from executive women who've been mistaken for assistants and asked to fetch coffee and snacks by male vendors who were in the room to sell to them. Often, these women shrug their shoulders at the vendors' mistakes. They've seen it all. But they don't forget. Is it any wonder so many women approach sales interactions with their guard up?

Just as we continually upgrade our software to stay current, we must upgrade our customer experiences to stay relevant. In a consumer economy dominated by women, new skills are needed. Selling is no longer about conquest and combat, as it was when sales strategies were largely based on men selling to other men. Nor is it about ignoring people, like the sales associate I almost met in Atlantic City. Today, it's about inspiring people to buy from you. And learning what that looks like with women customers is opportunity number one. You're about to gain a deeper understanding of the perspectives, life experiences, and communication styles of the world's biggest consumer market. Many of the strategies we'll cover in this book will enhance your male customers' experience too. Winning the business of women isn't about excluding men; it's about excluding stereotypes and elevating the customer experience.

These perspectives will help you stay one step ahead of millennial (born approximately between the years 1980 and 2000) and Gen Z (born after 2000) customers of both genders, since many values that have historically been associated with women—like wanting to buy from companies that make the world a better place in some way—now apply to the younger generations.

In the same way that women's needs have driven changes for men in the workplace (for example, maternity leave is fast becoming parental leave so that men can take it too), women are driving changes in the consumer marketplace that younger generations of both genders not only appreciate but also expect. A good rule of thumb is this: if you want to know where the market is going, follow the women. Women are the leading indicators for what people want.

## THE "G" WORD

Gender is a topic we don't discuss in the context of sales and customer experiences very often, so allow me to take a moment to clarify how we'll talk about it. All women—and men—are individuals, and should be treated as such. Women are not all the same, just as men are not all the same. Yet, each of us is born into a society that recognizes two primary gender "cultures": the male culture and the female culture. The gender culture in which we grow up impacts how we're socialized and interact with the world, including the communication styles we use.[2] The descriptions in this book should be viewed as tendencies, not absolutes, that are based on the aspects of female culture that can affect women's perceptions of sales interactions.

Here's an analogy for gender culture: Imagine you were planning a vacation to Italy and decided to learn everything you could about Italian culture. You study Italian history and modern society; you practice helpful tourist phrases in Italian; you learn expectations for customs such as tipping and hailing a cab. You're happy to put in the work because you know the knowledge will enrich your experience. And yet, when your plane touches down in Rome, you would never expect every Italian to behave the same way. After all, it's a nation of 60 million personalities. However, your preparation has provided you with a valuable foundation that allows you to communicate more easily, confidently, and ultimately, successfully. That's the spirit in which this book is written. It's a guide to the cultural conditions of modern women that will help you exceed their expectations as customers. But it bears repeating: every customer is an individual, first and foremost, and should be treated as such.

Let me also clarify the language I'll be using so we're on the same page. I use the term *sales professional* to describe all of us who work with customers for a living. I recognize that few people use that title in real life. However, whether you manage a sales team, run a dude ranch, work in retail, or are an independent business owner, your success depends on customers agreeing to pay for your products and services. Hence, we're all sales professionals.

For the sake of simplicity, I will use the word *customer* to refer to women consumers in general, though depending on your industry, you may call them guests, patients, clients, community members, fans, or something else altogether.

## THIS ISN'T A WOMEN'S ISSUE—IT'S A STRATEGIC ISSUE

Now that we have our language squared away, let's set the stage for our discussion. The economic opportunity with women buyers is often viewed as a "women's issue" and not a business issue. This is a mistake. I've seen many companies—and sales professionals—limit their growth potential by thinking this way. Hosting an event for International Women's Day, for example, is laudable and important, but it's not a substitute for a long-term growth strategy. That requires a longer view, and the tools and techniques in this book are designed to help you get there. You'll find:

- Practical strategies to increase your customers' emotional engagement
- The Four Motivators Framework for creating experiences that appeal to women customers
- Communication "watch-outs" to avoid
- Best practices from leading brands, businesses, and sales professionals
- A road map of the biggest trends driving women's buying patterns
- Activities at the end of every chapter to help jump-start your growth (also included as an appendix)
- A Monday Morning Action Plan to create a long-term strategy for your business

Winning women's business is about creating *inclusive* customer experiences that incorporate the perspectives of the people who drive most of the buying. Our world is changing fast, but one thing remains constant: women's domination of consumer spending. That fact alone provides a valuable compass for navigating, and winning, the future. So as we move forward, keep in mind that this is not simply a women's issue—it's a strategic issue, and it's huge. Let's get started.

## CHAPTER 1

# YOUR BIGGEST GROWTH MARKET IS ALREADY HERE

f I were to ask you to name the world's biggest growth markets, what would you say?

China?

India?

You'd be right with either of those answers, because they're both major growth markets. But there's another massive one that's right here at home, no matter where you call home, and that's women. Thanks to women's increased educational attainment, labor-force participation, and earning power, women are now considered one of the world's largest growth markets. A *Harvard Business Review* article put it this way: "In aggregate, women represent a growth market bigger than China and India combined—more than twice as big."[1]

I've dedicated most of my career to studying women in the consumer economy. It's not a typical job, and you can imagine the jokes I hear when I tell people what I do. They usually revolve around the idea that women's spending is trivial and even frivolous, as if women were only interested in shoes, handbags, and sparkly things. While there is nothing wrong with any of these purchases, this stereotype does a disservice to women and is a potential lost opportunity for sales professionals.

"You should see what my wife does to my credit card!" is a comment I hear often. When someone says this to me, I just smile, and then tell that person the real reasons women drive so much consumer spending. That's when the jokes stop, and the conversations get a lot more interesting.[2]

In virtually every society in the world, women are primary caregivers for both children and the elderly. Are there exceptions? Sure, but this is a role that remains overwhelmingly female. As primary caregivers, women typically assume responsibility for buying on behalf of everyone in their households. They're the chief purchasing officers for their families. You already know that mothers buy on behalf of their children and that women buy for spouses and partners. That's just the beginning. Women buy on behalf of their older parents, their in-laws, their businesses, and often, friends, neighbors, and community organizations, since women volunteer at higher rates than men do across all age groups and educational levels.[3]

Adding up all this spending and decision-making on behalf of others is how we arrive at the reality of women's buying power and influence, which is felt across industries. For example, women make 80 percent of the health-care decisions for their families.[4] When you earn the business and loyalty of one woman, you have an opportunity to reach the other people in her household, as well as her social and business networks, because she is buying on behalf of so many others. Women are the gateway to everybody else.

## WELCOME TO THE WOMEN'S MULTIPLIER EFFECT

As gateways to other people, women have what I call a *multiplier effect* on sales.[5] Even when a woman isn't paying for something with her own money, she is typically a strong influencer—or veto vote—behind somebody else's purchase. All around us, we see examples of how this plays out. For instance, if a husband and wife look at a model home and the woman doesn't like it, the couple is unlikely to buy it.

This multiplier effect has several dimensions that can impact your sales success. One aspect of it, for example, is the way women are prime drivers of word-of-mouth publicity (which now includes social sharing online) for the people and companies with which they do business. This is because in female culture, women tend to talk about their buying experiences with one another, routinely discussing topics such as what they bought, where they bought it, what kind of deal they got (if they got one), and what kind of service they received, if it was memorable. Typically, men don't talk to their male friends about these topics with the same frequency and depth that women do.

Women talk about these subjects because they know their female friends usually have the same responsibilities they do in terms of provisioning and procurement for the household. Women also share the same pressures to meet cultural standards for grooming, personal appearance, meal preparation, home cleanliness, and child-rearing, to name just a handful of society's "gendered" expectations. As such, they often feel that it's nothing less than their duty to inform their friends about great resources and warn them away from bad experiences, in the spirit of being helpful. This is one reason a happy female customer can generate a huge rate of return in word-of-mouth publicity. She represents a broad range of other potential customers.

Another aspect of the multiplier effect is that women often assume responsibility for marking life's milestones within a household or family—or even an office—and all the celebrations, events, and gift giving that go along with them, from baby showers to birthdays to funerals. These milestones are catalysts for spending and marketplace engagement.

Women also perform huge amounts of emotional labor. This phrase has more than one definition, but for our purposes I'm using the term *emotional labor* to refer to the invisible activities involved in caregiving and maintaining social relationships. These include actions such as anticipating and accommodating other people's emotional needs; organizing social activities that bring people together; remembering other people's appointments and whereabouts; keeping track of other people's sizes, favorite foods, and general likes and dislikes; and demonstrating a sustained interest in the well-being of others.

Emotional labor is a woman saying to her partner, "Next Thursday is the first anniversary of Tom's wife's death. We should invite him over for dinner so he's not alone that night." This sentiment sounds simple, but when you break it down, it's like a five-act play in which a woman is directing, producing, and starring. The first act is remembering the anniversary of the death. The second act is making a plan to invite Tom for dinner. The third act is reaching out to Tom and inviting him. The fourth act is deciding what's going to happen that evening (dinner at home or in a restaurant). And the fifth act is executing the evening's activities. Many women will tell you they have several mental checklists in their heads running at all times, and while they won't call these checklists *emotional labor*, that's often what they are.

All of this means that even if your customer doesn't tell you how busy she is, you can assume she has a lot going on and will be grateful if you make it easy and convenient to do business with you. Do men engage in emotional labor too? Yes, of course. However, studies show that women engage in substantially more of these activities throughout their lives, and moreover, it is a cultural expectation that they do so.[6] From a buying perspective, the implication is that women's "radars" are permanently scanning for products and services that the people close to them might need or want, and this impacts how they approach the marketplace. I sometimes think entire industries would collapse overnight if women stopped being so thoughtful. Consider the impact to the greeting card industry alone!

## AN ECONOMIC SNAPSHOT

While women have long held the role of gatekeepers for their households, they've unleashed a tidal wave of change in our economy in a very short time. When you consider that as recently as 1974 it was difficult for an unmarried woman in the United States to get a credit card in her own name—until the Equal Credit Opportunity Act was passed—the pace of change in two generations has been nothing less than astonishing. Let's look at a few eye-opening stats that provide context for how your business and sales strategies can adapt.

*Women Dominate Higher Education.* Women earn the majority of associate's degrees, bachelor's degrees, master's degrees, and even doctoral degrees in the United States.[7] This is part of a global shift: women are outpacing men's higher education participation in many world markets.[8] Education has catapulted women into fields that were traditionally dominated by men, like law, medicine, and science, to name just a few.[9] If we consider that someone's educational attainment is a good predictor of his or her future earning power, the data on graduation rates shows us that women's status as "alpha consumers" will likely continue for the next two to three decades at least. This means women aren't just the customers of today; they're the customers of the future. Here's how the numbers break down in the United States:

- bachelor's degrees: 57 percent earned by women
- master's degrees: 59 percent earned by women
- doctoral degrees: 53 percent earned by women

*Women in the Workforce: The Biggest Revolution of Our Time.* Women's participation in the labor force has been one of the most sweeping and peaceful revolutions in modern history, impacting every facet of society. Stereotypes to the contrary, most mothers of young children now work outside the home. In fact, 70 percent of women with children under eighteen participate in the US labor force, and the overwhelming majority of these women (75 percent) work full time.[10] This is an enormous change from 1975, when less than half of all mothers with children under eighteen were in the labor force. Despite the numbers, employed women still perform more unpaid household chores and caregiving responsibilities than employed men,[11] which means that providing them with convenient ways to conduct business with you is crucial to staying relevant with this market.

At the other end of the age spectrum, more people than ever are working into their later years. Because women have a longer life expectancy than men and typically shoulder more eldercare responsibilities, we can expect they will be a significant part of this growing population of older workers, which will have an impact on both their consumer needs and time constraints.

*More Women Are Breadwinners.* What does a breadwinner look like? If you're thinking of a man in a suit, it's time to update that image and make it more inclusive of women. Mothers are the primary or sole earners for 40 percent of households with children under eighteen.[12] This represents a sea change in our society, and there are several factors behind it. Not only are women earning more degrees and engaged in the labor force in large numbers, but there are more single-parent households in our society, and women overwhelmingly dominate these households.[13]

*Women Control Wealth.* Women control 51 percent of personal wealth.[14] They are wealth creators due to their workforce participation and entrepreneurialism, and wealth inheritors because of their longer life expectancies. Both of these factors impact women's decision-making and financial needs. Forty percent of new entrepreneurs are women,[15] and women-owned businesses account for 39 percent of all US firms.[16] We will hear from women business owners throughout these pages and learn the innovative ways they serve their own customers.

*Women Hold Most Management and Professional Positions.* Women account for 52 percent of all workers employed in management, professional, and related occupations.[17] One implication of this number is that B2B sales are now increasingly inclusive of women. Many forward-looking businesses are fielding more diverse account teams to reflect the customer bases they serve.

*Women Dominate the Big Social Networks.* Females are the dominant users of Facebook, Instagram, Twitter, Pinterest,[18] and Snapchat.[19] We all know that social sharing has never been more important for businesses in terms of publicity, reputation, and sales. What we don't often hear is that women are the primary users on most of the biggest social networks. This is another key aspect of their "multiplier effect" on businesses.

*Caregiving.* Globally, women undertake the majority of unpaid care, including housework, childcare, and eldercare.[20] The numbers vary by country, but overwhelmingly, women's unpaid work functions as a second or third job that must be maintained along with any paid work outside the home. This is one of the biggest differences in life experience that women bring to the table as customers: they're often evaluating the wants and needs of other people as they make buying decisions, and juggling multiple caregiving responsibilities.[21]

These stats paint an extraordinary picture of women's economic impact. Yet women are still absent from leadership positions in the corporate world. While women make up the majority of consumers, men make up 95 percent of CEOs for S&P 500 companies, and they almost always lead male-dominated management teams.[22] Women-founded companies (in which all founders are female) receive only 2 percent of venture capital funding.[23] As these numbers show, there's still an enormous gender gap between women buyers and the leadership of the companies that market and sell to them. My philosophy is that whenever there's a gap, there's an opportunity to fill it. That's why we're here. Closing this gap with insights and information will help put you one step ahead of the competition and create more satisfied customers.

## KEY TAKEAWAYS

- Women are one of the world's biggest growth markets, and meeting their needs as customers is key to succeeding in the modern economy.
- Women have a multiplier effect on the businesses and sales professionals that serve them well.
- Understanding the pace of women's educational and economic progress is fundamental to staying relevant with this market.

## ACTIVATING YOUR INSIGHTS

- If you were to rank your business on a scale of 1 to 10 on its effectiveness in connecting with modern women consumers, with 10 being the highest, what number would you give? Use this number as a benchmark for future progress.
- How have you seen differences in gender culture play out in

your own customer interactions? What did you learn from these experiences?

- Categorize your customer data by gender. Can you identify specific buying patterns and preferences by examining the information this way?

## CHAPTER 2

# WHAT SELLING LOOKS LIKE NOW

Quick: think of a buying experience you've had with a sales-person that was so great you told people about it.

Still thinking?

Chances are, you're drawing a blank, because from a customer perspective, sales experiences are generally bad. Maybe not out-rageously bad, but *lackluster*. Ineffective. Forgettable. And this has created an enormous opportunity for anyone who isn't.

In my work, I spend my days asking women (and many men too) how they buy, what they buy, from whom they buy, and why they buy from certain people and businesses but not others. When I ask people to share a story with me about a great cus-tomer experience with a sales professional, I'm often met with a blank stare. "Give me more time," they'll say. "I'm sure I can come up with something."

Usually, they don't.

E-commerce has changed our perspective on buying in real life (IRL). It's become the unlikely new benchmark for flawless, *personal* service, to the extent that some women feel their online buying experiences are higher quality than their face-to-face purchase interactions. Partly, this is because e-commerce transac-tions eliminate many of the variables encountered in traditional sales situations. Consider a routine retail transaction: a woman is in the market for a new weatherproof jacket. She searches on Amazon.com and finds the exact color and size she needs. She reads the customer reviews of the product and feels confident enough to place her order. Once she does, she gets an immediate email confirmation with a thank-you message, and she's notified when the product leaves the warehouse. She gets the jacket conveniently at home, followed by a message asking for her feedback after the purchase. Later, she receives personalized recommendations for other items she might like, based on her selection of that jacket.

Now, imagine this woman walks into a store looking for the same jacket. The variables she encounters are endless. She may or may not be greeted; she may or may not get eye contact; she may or may not be actively helped; she may or may not work with an associate who has any knowledge of the product she's interested in; the jacket she wants may or may not be in stock; and she may or may not be followed up with, even when she asks an associate to tell her if the jacket can be found at another location in her size. She never hears from the store again. She buys it somewhere else instead.

*It doesn't need to be this way.* Here's what should have happened if the traditional store were more competitive with the online customer experience: the customer walks into a store looking for the weatherproof jacket. A sales associate gives her a friendly welcome and starts a conversation by asking about her needs. She tells him she's about to go on her first hiking trip and that she wants the right gear. The associate finds out more about her plans and learns that she will be camping too. Before you know it, he's recommended a jacket with thicker insulation, as well as wool socks and a backpack large enough to accommodate her supplies. The weatherproof jacket is out of stock in the color she wants, but he orders it for her and has it shipped directly to her home. The customer learns about products she didn't even know she needed and walks out of the store with more than she had intended to buy. The jacket arrives at her home a few days later, and she feels not only satisfied with her purchase but also thrilled with the retailer that provided help beyond what she'd asked.

In this scenario, the traditional retailer was able to sell more products than the online retailer because the sales associate was proactive with questions and suggestions, and provided the help and attention the customer needed. The power of asking "why" and not just "what" is a key advantage for anyone selling IRL.

Unfortunately, this is too often the exception. Some women avoid the in-person customer experience altogether due to the mere thought that an IRL sales experience might not go well, might not be efficient, might not be productive, or might even be offensive in some way. As one woman told me, "In some places, you wouldn't know who worked there if they came up and bit you—you feel like you're on your own." This explains the growing reliance on crowdsourced review sites, and it's upped the ante for every human being who earns a living by engaging customers. For sales professionals, it's critical to maintain such a strong reputation for consistently great service that people seek you out because you've eliminated a variable for them: They know they'll have a great experience with you.

Chances are, whatever you sell, there's a cheaper and/or more convenient option available somewhere else. This is why it's more important than ever to provide memorable person-to-person engagement. Research shows that 77 percent of consumers will choose a human over a digital capability when seeking advice.[1] And yet it seems that many companies have invested in technology while letting the "human side" of selling wither. This is one reason great IRL customer experiences are still the exception and not the rule, despite our state-of-the-art communication tools.

From a woman's standpoint, many sales experiences still fall into one of two extremes:

← ———————————————————————————————— →

**"Do you even want my money?"**        **"Stop bothering me."**

The sweet spot is somewhere in the middle. At the risk of stating the obvious, people flock to businesses that hit the sweet spot with great customer experiences. Think of all those friendly people in the colorful T-shirts at Apple stores. Are they selling? Sure, they are. Does it feel like they're selling? No. It feels like they're helping. They're educating. They're offering suggestions, fixing problems, answering questions, and generally making you feel great about improving your life with their products. Visiting their stores is so enjoyable that the Fifth Avenue location in New York City is open around the clock, because why should anyone have to wait to get a shot of Apple inspiration?

One young woman told me that she loved visiting Apple stores because, "I am surrounded by people who are so knowledgeable,

I feel empowered." This is quite a statement when one considers how easy it would be for Apple to make its customers feel stupid, since few people know how the products work and their customer service people have the title of *geniuses*.

No matter. People walk out of an Apple store feeling smarter than when they walked in, and that is a feat of emotional engagement. The world's most technologically advanced company has embraced the human side of selling to phenomenal effect. Apple generates more sales per square foot in its stores than any other retailer. Yes, this is partly because their products are expensive, but no one can deny that customers flock to the company's brick-and-mortar experience as they do to few other retailers.

## SELLING: WHAT'S CHANGED AND WHAT HASN'T

Engaging women consumers as powerfully as Apple connects with its customers begins with understanding some important ways the selling landscape has changed:

1. *The balance of power has flipped.* The internet has fundamentally altered the balance of power between buyers and sellers. The company or sales professional no longer "owns" all the information about a product or service. Some customers feel they know more about the products they're interested in than the people selling them.
2. *Fast and easy have been redefined.* E-commerce, Amazon Prime, in-home digital assistants, voice technology, augmented

reality, apps, and on-demand businesses are just some of the innovations that have changed people's perceptions of convenience and speed, forcing sales professionals to compete with a differentiated offering.

3. *People need a reason to get off the couch.* In brick-and-mortar environments, such as stores and sales offices, the new imperative is to deliver the kind of personal, sensory-rich, and service-oriented experience that inspires people to leave their houses to seek it out.

The medical profession offers an interesting analogy for how things have changed for sales professionals. Imagine a physician whose patient walks into the exam room holding a stack of online research about her symptoms. Before the doctor has a chance to conduct her examination, the patient tells her she's come up with her own diagnosis, based on her research. The doctor listens to the patient before delivering her own point of view, which is based on years of medical training and practice.

In this scenario, the patient possesses information, while the physician possesses knowledge, subject-matter expertise, and the professional experience of working with thousands of other patients who've had similar symptoms. Yet because the patient has access to so much information, the conversation is different—and potentially longer and more dynamic—than it would have been pre-internet.

For sales professionals, the scenario is relatable. Often, women have already conducted some research before they meet with you.

They may have conducted extensive research if what you're selling has a high price tag or is "high stakes" from their point of view. They've read the reviews. They've looked on social media. They've watched videos made by other customers. They've compared options, checked prices, and maybe even learned all about your professional background on LinkedIn or your company website. In this new environment, the challenge is to add value to a process that the customer feels she has already partially, or wholly, completed. This can be a difficult adjustment to make, to be sure. And, yet, it feels good to know that many fundamentals have not changed:

1. *People will always want and need to buy things.* The need for selling is not going away any time soon; success means inspiring customers to buy from you instead of someone or somewhere else.

2. *It's exciting to buy from someone who believes in what he or she is selling.* This explains the happy "buzz" at Apple stores and the high frequency of employee/customer interactions within them. There's nothing more contagious than buying from someone who has passion for their work and believes in their products.

3. *Strong interpersonal skills go a long way.* As we have seen, our definition of good service has changed because of the new standards set by e-commerce, apps, and algorithms. This means that effective communication skills are more important than ever.

## KEY TAKEAWAYS

- Women's societal roles and increased education and wealth means that they are not only the primary consumers of today, but also the primary consumers of tomorrow.
- E-commerce has changed our expectations for buying IRL and increased the importance of strong interpersonal skills and customer engagement.
- Great sales experiences are still the exception and not the rule. This creates an enormous opportunity for those who can deliver valuable experiences to customers.

## ACTIVATING YOUR INSIGHTS

- Think about the best buying experience you've ever had with a sales professional. What did that professional do well that made the experience so memorable? What lessons can you apply to your own business based on that experience?
- Write down your favorite places to shop/buy/be a customer, including both e-commerce companies and traditional businesses. What are these companies doing well that you could adapt for your own business?

## CHAPTER 3

# THE FOUR MOTIVATORS FRAMEWORK

You want your customers to tell a story about their experience with you. What's the best way to ensure it's the story you want them to tell? Reverse engineer the customer experience to create a positive emotional outcome.

You don't have to look any further than the stock market to see how positive emotional outcomes can lead to positive financial outcomes. Generally speaking, when people feel positive and optimistic en masse, the stock market goes up. When they feel anxious, negative, or threatened en masse, it goes down. At an individual level, this happens during our customer interactions. It's how you make people feel that makes them want to work with you and buy from you.

Emotional outcomes are so essential that luxury automaker Lexus now measures them through a survey instrument. "Emotion is an important measure for loyalty," says Peggy Turner, vice president of Lexus guest retention and satisfaction. "People talk about customer satisfaction, but that's a given. We want to know: *How did we make the guest feel?*"

So, how does one reverse engineer a sales experience for a positive outcome? While every buyer is different, a good start is to recognize that customers often fall into two distinct buying styles: transactional and holistic. Transactional buying is known colloquially as the surgical strike. This is when you have a customer who thinks, *I know what I want. I just want to get it from you and get on with my life.*

Holistic buying refers to a "big picture" buying style in which the customer is engaged in multiple aspects of the experience beyond product and price.[1] These elements include such things as their enjoyment working with you, the appeal of your sales environment, and long-term considerations, such as service after the sale. Here's a snapshot of transactional versus holistic buying styles:

### Transactional vs. Holistic Buying

| Transactional Buying | Holistic Buying |
|---|---|
| Shop for a single item | Shop comprehensively—what else goes with this item? |
| Evaluating the product only | Evaluating the product *and* the sales experience, including the salesperson interaction |
| Thinking, *"Will this work for me?"* | Thinking, *"Will this work for everyone else too?"* |
| Lower expectations for attentive service | Higher expectations for attentive service |
| Information seekers | Information and *inspiration* seekers |

Someone can be a holistic buyer one moment and a transactional buyer the next. What "mode" that buyer is in when she's with you can depend on everything from how busy she is that day to how emotionally invested she is (or isn't) in your product. Frequently, women find themselves in a holistic buying mode for two reasons. First, because their role as chief purchasing officers for their households adds layers of complexity to their decision-making.

Women may be thinking about factors such as time constraints, due to the "second shift" of unpaid work they perform in their households and for their extended families. They're often considering other people's wants and needs and view buying decisions through those lenses. They may be thinking about the potential that they will have to return a purchase if something goes wrong—even when the product is for someone else in their household—and what that will mean in terms of further time expended, and perhaps a negative experience after the fact. So as they approach buying, women want their purchases to go right the first time and will look for ways to make these responsibilities as pleasant and productive as possible.

The second reason women are often holistic buyers is that from an early age, women are taught a "big picture" buying style. For example, a woman may think about buying not just a shirt, but an outfit; not just a main course, but side dishes and dessert; not just a bedspread, but matching sheets and pillows. This is why many women will be interested in learning about other products or services that "go with" what you're selling. This buying style has a highly practical aspect: it's more efficient, and often more satisfying, to buy complementary products together, rather than make separate trips or multiple transactions. Women also may perceive that the value of such purchases is higher, because the whole is greater than the sum of its parts.

If you master the experience for holistic buyers, you'll naturally please your transactional buyers too, by giving them an experience they may not have been looking for or expecting, but are happy to receive nonetheless. Appealing to holistic buyers means adjusting your style accordingly, with an approach I've developed called The Four Motivators® Framework.

## INTRODUCING THE FOUR MOTIVATORS FRAMEWORK

There are so many things you can't control about your work. To name just three: the economy, the pace of technology, and the weather. You could probably come up with fifty more. Happily, you are in control of what is arguably the most important factor of all: your customer's experience.

Based on more than a dozen years of consumer research, I've identified four key motivators that influence women's buying decisions. Following the framework of these four motivators will help you develop strategies to appeal to women consumers more effectively. Ideally, your customers want to feel:

- *connected* to you, your brand, and your business,
- *inspired* to buy from you,
- *confident* in their buying decision, and
- *appreciated* for their business.

These motivators can serve as your guidepost for winning women's business. While you may never hear a customer use these specific words, they are the positive emotional outcomes that can help you earn more sales and referrals when they're achieved. Throughout the rest of this book, you'll find dozens of strategies for activating the four motivators, which you can consider your "toolbox," to mix, match, and add to at will.

As a professional, you already know there is never one way to win someone's business. Sales is a different job every day, every hour, and with every customer. Success involves a combination of knowledge, savvy judgment, and your own personality and style. With that in mind, I've included tips and best practices from big businesses, small businesses, and individual sales professionals, all designed to inspire your creativity. To get your ideas flowing, let's start with a best practice from an unexpected source: a professional football team.

## BEST PRACTICE

## Minnesota Vikings
*Champions of Emotional Engagement*

Most people may not think of a professional football game as a *customer experience*, but the Minnesota Vikings sure do. In 2016, this National Football League team completed construction of U.S. Bank Stadium in Minneapolis, which was the site of Super Bowl 52 in 2018. In addition to building an architectural marvel, the organization made it a priority to create an inclusive fan experience at every touchpoint. A look at how one professional sports team delivers an experience that encompasses all four motivators is a compelling example for any business.

Most professional sports fans will never set foot in a stadium, which poses an interesting challenge for teams with global fan bases. "Only 4 percent of all the people in the world who call themselves Vikings fans will ever come into U.S. Bank Stadium," says Kevin Warren, chief operating officer for the Minnesota Vikings. "So when we are fortunate that a fan decides to spend their resources and come support us, we have to make sure that we capture their mind, their spirit, their heart and their soul by over-servicing them, because that might be the only time they ever enter our building. We need to create an experience that lasts for the remainder of their lives. It is an incredible responsibility."

Warren thinks big about the fan experience. He strives to make every game day at U.S. Bank Stadium so remarkable that it could inspire someone from out of town to move to Minnesota. He has what I would call radical empathy for fans. "When someone comes into our stadium, it is not only *them* coming in," says Warren. "They are bringing all these other people with them, in spirit, who are not physically present. When they go back home, they are either going to say, 'This was the best experience of my life,' or they will say it was an awful experience.

"That said," he continues, "we need to make sure that we have the proper food; that the seats are comfortable; that we accommodate any fan regardless of their income level or background; that we accommodate families; that we have merchandise and apparel for everyone, and that the apparel fits right; that we have places where women can breastfeed their children in privacy. We have built a sensory room in the stadium for young people who are dealing with autism and other sensory challenges. We want to make every member of our diverse fan base feel comfortable and enjoy what it means to be a member of the Minnesota Vikings."

The Vikings do an exceptional job of engaging with the various demographics within their fan base and, in particular, their female fans. Women make up 45 percent of the National Football League fan base[2] and nearly 50 percent of Vikings ticket holders.[3] It makes sense, then, that there is an emphasis on delivering experiences that delight this group and cater to their needs. For example, the Vikings made history by becoming the first team in the National Football League to place Mamava lactation pods in their stadium to provide private nursing areas for breastfeeding women. The pods were a hit: demand was so strong that the initiative was expanded to include a dedicated mother's room in the stadium. "Having witnessed the positive response and increased demand for the lactation suites, we strongly believed the addition of the Mother's Room was another critical step in building a family-friendly environment at U.S. Bank Stadium," says Warren.[4]

The organization has also been intentional about elevating the voices and participation of women within its business operations. In 2016, a women's advisory board of leading female executives (yours truly is on it) was formally created to maximize the team's engagement with women fans. The Vikings organization counts women among its senior leaders. A twenty-one-year veteran of the Vikings, Tami Hedrick, has a director-level role dedicated to driving full inclusiveness of women throughout the organization, both internally and externally, through an initiative called "Vikings Women." "It's a holistic approach to engaging women, who are integral to the Vikings' success," says Hedrick. There are Vikings Women events held regularly throughout the year; Vikings Women merchandise and apparel fills the team stores; and there are ongoing social media efforts to reach women fans. Hedrick and her team also run a year-round calendar of engagement and leadership activities for women in the Vikings organization.

The result of the Minnesota Vikings' inclusive strategy is the four motivators in action: women fans feel *connected*, *inspired*, *confident*, and *appreciated* because the organization

- *connects* through the visible way the team reaches out to women in the stadium, the community, and internally within its organization,
- *inspires* by creating an inclusive fan experience,
- *instills confidence* that attending a game will be worth the ticket price and effort to get there, and
- *shows appreciation* by offering amenities and accommodation for every type of fan . . . even newborns!

---

## BRINGING THE FOUR MOTIVATORS FRAMEWORK TO LIFE IN YOUR PHYSICAL SPACE

The Vikings activate the four motivators in multiple ways throughout their business, but one key focus is the intentionality they take with their physical space. This is something every business can work on. Stadiums notwithstanding, there are plenty of ways your physical environment can bring the four motivators to life, whether you operate a retail space or work in a professional office that customers visit.

The décor in professional offices is often overlooked, but it can make an enormous impression on how you're perceived. Scratched-up metal desks, bulging file cabinets, and bare walls can leave customers feeling that a business isn't current, or even competent. For proof of how much office design matters, look no further than the success of the co-working company WeWork. It's achieved a $20 billion market cap[5] (as of this writing) by not only tapping into the desire for flexible workspaces, but also by elevating the décor, ambiance, and community feel of shared offices, creating spaces that are so appealing people are willing to pay a premium to sit in them all day.

Everything in your physical space is either a customer-experience builder or a detractor. Consider stores: at their most basic, they're four walls and a ceiling. What makes some of them so enticing that we want to experience them again and again, while others we only visit under duress? It's the environment, of course, that stew of ambiance created by lighting, textures, colors, merchandise, scent, cleanliness, sound, comfort, and the energy given off by employees. Women especially tend to notice and value the details in retail environments.

As one woman told me, "When I walk into Whole Foods, I feel an immediate reaction. I'm not sure if it's serotonin or dopamine. The store is so colorful and organized—it's a total 360-degree feel-good experience."

With so much of our time spent staring at devices, compelling physical environments are more important now than ever. Just as movie-theater owners are creating new experiences by providing amenities such as restaurant-quality table service and pre-reserved reclining seats, every business with a physical environment must evolve its space so that women feel connected, inspired, confident, and appreciated. How do you get started? Here are four important principles to follow:

1. *Provide a sensory experience.* For the most part, it's still difficult to touch, taste, or smell anything through a screen. This means brick-and-mortar businesses have what I call a "home-court advantage": the opportunity to engage all five senses within a physical environment.

2. *Bring your brand to life.* Research shows that a strong brand and physical environment make a significant contribution to converting sales, even when a transaction is eventually registered online.[6] People who feel inspired by a great in-person experience may ultimately decide to execute their purchase at a company's website after they've left the physical store or place of business. This brings a new imperative for stores and professional offices to become the physical embodiment of a brand experience, more than simply a place to buy things.

3. *Demonstrate hospitality.* Physical acts, such as having staff members walk a customer down an aisle (instead of merely pointing them in a direction), offering refreshments, and engaging them in conversations that help them make better

buying decisions, leave customers with an indelible memory of appreciation, long after the purchase was made.

4. *Facilitate show-and-tell.* Most of us learned about the power of show-and-tell as kids. The concept can be applied successfully across all kinds of physical spaces. Sephora is a great example of a brand that leverages show-and-tell. The brand's stores are a playground for experimentation and a radical departure from a century of locked-behind-a-counter beauty experiences. In an industry where trial is such a crucial part of the purchasing decision, the experience at Sephora leaves customers feeling confident about committing to a purchase in a crowded category. We'll learn more about how Sephora wins women's business in chapter 6.

Maybe you're thinking, *Well, sure, Sephora can create an engaging experience for women, because they sell beauty products. I don't sell female-specific products. What can I do?* Let's look at the transformation of a truck stop for more insights into the value of strategically incorporating the four motivators in a physical space.

## BEST PRACTICE

## Pilot Flying J
### *When a Truck Stop Is Worth the Stop*

When I say the words "truck stop," what image comes to mind? I guarantee it's not the one you'll see when you visit the newly redesigned travel centers from Pilot Flying J. Pilot Travel Centers LLC, better known as Pilot Flying J, is the largest operator of travel centers (also known as truck stops) in North America. Many people started paying closer attention to the company in 2017, when Berkshire Hathaway, led by Warren Buffett, announced that it would be making a significant investment in the firm.[7] The Tennessee-based company has 750 locations spread across forty-four states and six Canadian provinces that cater to both professional truck drivers and "four wheelers"—regular car drivers like you and me. Most of us "four wheelers" don't think about making a roadside stop until we need one. But what if a travel center was so appealing that you looked forward to stopping in?

Pilot Flying J recently embarked on a five-year, $500 million customer-experience makeover to broaden its appeal to a growing customer base that includes more women and "four wheelers" than ever before: traveling families, married truck-driving teams, and business travelers. I toured one of the company's newly redesigned Pilot travel centers in Lebanon, Tennessee, and what I saw was the four motivators in action.

"People want to emotionally connect with how they feel in your store," says Whitney Haslam Johnson, chief experience officer for Pilot Flying J, who served as my tour guide. Haslam Johnson is a member of the Haslam family that founded, and still runs, the business. "We don't want it to feel like a truck stop," she says. "Life is hard enough, busy enough, crazy enough. How can we make it easy and efficient for you?"

Like U.S. Bank Stadium, the refurbished Pilot Travel Centers are designed to create a positive emotional connection with every customer who walks in the door. However, unlike a football stadium, Pilot Flying J stores must cater to the needs of transactional buyers—people who want to get in and out quickly so they can get back on the road—as well as holistic buyers—people who might come into the store to engage in the only relaxing break, hot meal, and social interaction they'll have all day (these are often professional truck drivers). For our purposes, we'll focus on the changes made in the store to enhance the experience for the four-wheel crowd, which increasingly includes women.

Throughout history, food has been a conduit for emotions, and in the new Pilot Flying J stores, food offerings are front and center—only not the kind you would imagine from a "truck stop." The first thing you see when you walk in the door is a "chef," an employee wearing a chef's smock, who is standing in an open kitchen, stirring large pots on a stove and personally serving hot meals to customers. After absorbing that pleasant surprise, you hear the unmistakable sound and notice the scent of coffee bean grinders. Pilot Flying J has installed bean-to-cup coffee machines, which means that every cup of coffee is made with freshly ground beans. During each morning's rush hour, a "coffee host" stands nearby to assist customers in making selections.

Fruit and healthy foods, such as salads and wraps, are in prime position at the store's entrance, under the brand's label, PJ Fresh. LED lighting brightens the display cases and makes the merchandise pop. The lighting sounds like a small thing, but it's a big thing: it makes the store feel bright, modern, and fresh.

The attention to detail extends to the restrooms, which are a critical amenity for women. "If the restroom experience is bad, we may lose a customer," says Haslam Johnson. "It's their first impression. When we look at customer feedback, we know that the bathroom is really important for women and people traveling with children." I toured the bathroom and saw a warm, immaculately clean space filled with Italian glass and tile, a full-length mirror, hooks for hanging bags and purses, and child seats. I noticed the sign for the women's bathroom wasn't a sign at all: it was a large photo of a woman at the wheel of a car, hair blowing in the breeze.

Another element Pilot Flying J has invested in is LED lighting in both its parking lots and its canopies to create a well-lit atmosphere and increase safety and comfort. The company has also invested in buying real estate near highway exits. As Haslam Johnson puts it, "No one wants to exit and then drive for miles in the dark." These are the kind of innovations that show women that you're committed to providing them with a positive experience. When you incorporate insights from women, such as safety concerns, you elevate the experience for everyone. After all, men want to be safe too.

To complete the customer experience, Pilot Flying J has the goal of sending off every customer with a personal goodbye. The store's general manager, Hunter Brock, describes it this way: "We make sure there's a greeting when you walk in, a departing comment when you leave, and a conversation in the middle."

The newly redesigned stores at Pilot Flying J are an example of the four motivators in action. Through their physical space, Pilot Flying J

- *connects* by having staff members greet customers as they walk through the door and say goodbye as they leave,

- *inspires* by providing an unexpectedly high level of food and drink choices, cleanliness, and in-store ambiance,
- *instills confidence* by lighting travel centers well and locating them close to highway exits, so customers know they won't have to drive too far off the road to get there, and
- *shows appreciation* for its customers by providing healthy food options, immaculate restrooms with thoughtful amenities, and women-specific merchandise on store shelves.

By looking at practical examples from industry leaders like Pilot Flying J, you'll be able to use your creativity to infuse the four motivators into your own business. The next four chapters will provide you with dozens of tools and techniques to make your customers feel more connected, inspired, confident, and appreciated.

## KEY TAKEAWAYS

- Customers often fall into two different buying styles: transactional and holistic. By aligning the buying experience for holistic buyers, you're likely to increase the appeal to women consumers, who often find themselves in this mode. You'll also be giving transactional buyers an experience they didn't expect but are happy to receive.

- The Four Motivators Framework can serve as your guidepost for creating positive emotional outcomes for your customers. Ideally, customers want to feel
  - *connected* to you, your brand, and your business,
  - *inspired* to buy from you,
  - *confident* in their buying decisions, and
  - *appreciated* for their business.
- The Minnesota Vikings and Pilot Flying J show us that providing an inclusive experience for women enhances the experience for every customer.

## ACTIVATING YOUR INSIGHTS

- Thinking about your own business and sales style, which motivators are your greatest strengths? Which need the most work?
  - My ability to connect
  - My ability to inspire
  - My ability to make customers feel confident
  - My proactivity in showing appreciation
- Imagine your customer is talking to a friend. Your customer tells her friend, "You *have* to work with [YOU], because \_\_\_\_ _____." What are the reasons you'd like the customer to give? How many can you come up with that don't involve price?

- Evaluate your business environment by seeing it through the lens of women customers. Answer the following questions, which reflect some of the things women may be noticing when they enter your place of business:
    - Does this place feel bright and modern?
    - Is the space clean?
    - Did I get a friendly welcome when I walked in?
    - Do the people here make me feel comfortable (i.e., are they polite and respectful)?
    - Are there any women working here?
    - Is there a place for me and/or my companions to sit down?
    - Do they cater to people with kids?
    - Do they show an interest in helping me?
    - Do the people here seem knowledgeable and trustworthy?
    - Do they offer good value for the price?
    - Can I count on them if something goes wrong with my purchase?
    - Would I want to come back here?
    - Do I feel compelled to tell my friends they need to come here?

CHAPTER 4

# MOTIVATOR #1: CONNECTED

*Create an Emotional Connection with Your Customers*

As a sales professional, you're a crucial part of your customers' buying experience just as much as, or even more than, the products and services you represent. Our first motivator, *connected*, is all about creating strong connections with your customers.

I've never once met anyone who has said, "My goal is to alienate my customers." Everyone I meet has the best intentions to treat customers equally well and believes in their heart that they do. But misunderstandings can happen that are sometimes rooted in the different life experiences men and women bring to the table. What follows are composites of three classic connection "killers" I've heard repeatedly from women buyers. As you read them, ask yourself: *Would these situations happen with male customers?*

## THE UNWANTED COMPLIMENT

A young woman walks into a small furniture store to look at a sofa she's spied in the window. The place is empty except for a lone employee, who stands up and greets her by saying, "You just made my day. I love it when a beautiful woman comes into my store." The salesperson thinks he is establishing rapport by paying her a compliment. He assumes all women want to hear that they're beautiful.

The compliment has the opposite effect on the customer. She freezes and is immediately uncomfortable. In her view, a comment on her appearance from a male stranger in an empty store is inappropriate and unwanted. It has nothing to do with buying a sofa. She leaves the store, and he tells himself she wasn't serious about buying. She gets a new sofa somewhere else.

*What went wrong:* The sales professional lost his customer at hello. He was trained on the features and benefits of every product in the store, but in the end it didn't matter. He failed to connect with this customer because he mistakenly believed that flattering her looks would be a good icebreaker. Understanding how to use compliments in customer interactions is important. It's not that compliments in general are unwelcome; it's that context, judgment, and language matter, particularly for women buyers. Did the sales professional intend for his comment to make her uncomfortable? No. But he hasn't spent a lifetime as a woman, being judged on appearances; thus, his perspective is completely different from hers. In this context, it would have been wiser for him to compliment her great choice of sofa instead. When in doubt about whether a compliment may be received well, take the "When in Doubt" test on page 50.

## THE OVER-SHARER

A woman walks into a luxury car dealership to test-drive and buy (she hopes) the car she's been researching online. She feels great when she realizes a female salesperson will be taking her on the test-drive. While she's driving the short distance, the salesperson establishes that they're both mothers of young children and starts talking about her recent divorce and her ex-husband's unwillingness to pay childcare. The customer is not interested in the sales associate's personal life and resents being forced to listen to her problems while in the car. The sales associate feels she is creating a bond with a fellow mother by sharing her personal story. She thinks, *Bonding is what women do, and now this customer has a reason to relate to me.*

By the end of the test-drive, the sales associate is still talking about her ex-husband, and the client is so exasperated she doesn't buy the new car because it would mean spending hours with the salesperson to execute the contract. She leaves and doesn't come back to the dealership. The salesperson wrongly assumes this woman was a "tire kicker" and doesn't realize her poor interpersonal skills drove her to a competitor, where she bought the very same car—no test-drive needed.

*What went wrong:* The customer was looking for a new car, not a new friend. This salesperson failed to walk the line between connecting with her customer by finding something in common and chasing her away by over-sharing personal information. We'll cover how to walk that fine line between "too much" and "not enough" through what I call the "boomerang strategy" on page 70.

## THE "NO QUESTIONS ASKED" BAD LISTENER

A mature woman sits down for an introductory phone call with a prospective financial advisor. Right off the bat, the advisor talks nonstop about his experience, his perspective on the market, and the pros and cons of specific financial products. He talks so much she can't interject a word, and after what feels like forever, she starts to tune him out. He has yet to ask her a single question about her goals or what she's looking for, and he is talking about products that are irrelevant to her needs. She cuts the call short and hangs up the phone, and he never hears from her again. He is left with the impression that she wasn't serious about engaging an advisor. She was.

*What went wrong:* This advisor spent too much time talking about himself and not enough time listening to his customer. Little did he know, this customer had decades of investing experience. His intention was to establish his credentials, but by dominating the conversation for so long and not asking questions early enough, he conveyed that if he were her advisor, she wouldn't be listened to or taken seriously. Active listening is key to winning in the women's market for any sales professional, and we'll cover multiple strategies for demonstrating this skill.

Each of these well-intentioned professionals had hoped to connect with his or her customers, and the customers had hoped to buy something. The sales professionals were unable to engage—and subsequently earn the business—because their ideas about how to connect with women were based on stereotypes, such as the idea that complimenting a woman on her looks is sure to win her over, or that aggressively displaying one's expertise is more important than listening. To effectively engage with modern women, we need to drop the stereotypes and learn what it really takes to connect. Here are some old assumptions to avoid:

- *Don't assume your customer is married, no matter her age or motherhood status.* Marriage rates are lower than they've ever been, due to factors such as high divorce rates, the cultural acceptance of cohabitating, and the increase in diverse, nontraditional family structures.

- *Don't assume that if your customer is married, she has the same last name as her spouse.* Many women keep their maiden names upon marriage.

- *Don't assume your married customer is not the breadwinner.* As we see in the numbers mentioned in the previous chapter, women are increasingly the primary income earners for their households.

- *Don't assume her partner or spouse is a man.* In the United States, same-sex marriage is legal in all fifty states.

- *Don't assume that all married women are mothers.* There are more adults than ever who do not have kids; there are also many who have them later in life. I've interviewed women who were mistaken for their children's nannies or even their grandmothers.

To help you in this area even further, here are some of the conversational "watch-outs" to avoid:

- When you find out a woman is childless, don't probe for reasons why, unless the information is needed to help her make a buying decision. Otherwise, respect her privacy in this area. Some women are childless by chance, and others are childless by choice. One way to respectfully learn about your customers' lifestyles—male or female—is to address topics such as what a typical day looks like for them, who lives in their households, or who else might use a product they're interested in buying.
- Don't say, "I guess you're more of a career person, right?" to a woman who doesn't have kids, for the same reasons as above.
- If you meet a woman who tells you she has one child, do not ask, "Don't you want your child to have a brother or sister?"

Regardless of your good intentions, do your best to avoid making comments that your customers could interpret as judgments about their personal lives.

## TAKE THE "WHEN IN DOUBT" TEST

All of these comments fail my "When in Doubt" test for personal remarks: this is an inclusivity test in which you ask yourself, *Would I say this to a man?* Our furniture salesman from the beginning of this chapter would fail this test, because it's unlikely he would ever comment on a male customer's attractiveness. It's also unlikely someone would say, "I guess you're more of a career person" to a man with a job. While there are no definitive rules on these matters, here's a helpful guideline: *If you wouldn't say something to a male customer in a million years, think twice before saying it to a woman.* Of course, there are exceptions—especially when it comes to appearance-related compliments in the fashion and beauty industries—but the bottom line is that your customer wants to feel that you're helping her make the best choice and not judging her on aspects of her life that have nothing to do with what you're selling.

Now that we've covered some of the "watch-outs," what should be done instead? What are the modern protocols for connecting with women buyers? The pages ahead will give you strategies for enhancing your connection, and best practices from some of the individuals and companies that do it best. There's no end to the possibilities for creating deeper and longer-lasting customer connections. For instance, let's look at how one extraordinary Chicago dental practice connects with its patients.

**BEST PRACTICE**

## Always There Dental Care
*Connecting Against All Odds*

Everyone remembers being afraid of going to the dentist as a kid. For many people, that fear never goes away. Imagine what life must be like for dentists, whose livelihoods depend on building such strong connections with patients that they're willing to overcome their fears to come back on a regular basis.

Women make 80 percent of health-care decisions for their families.[1] The decision to settle on a long-term health-care provider, like a dentist, is based on many factors, from insurance acceptance to office location, reputation, and, naturally, the quality of the patient experience. Scott Stiffle, DDS, founded the Chicago-based dental practice Always There Dental Care in 1983. It's a practice that doesn't just have patients; it has *fans* who sometimes stop by to hang out at the office—even when they don't have an appointment—because the atmosphere and people are so much fun. Is this typical? No. Do *you* hang out at your dentist's office?

Stiffle, known to his patients as Dr. Scott, connects in a unique way—through music. Specifically, rock music. Walking into his practice is like entering a party in which everyone is glad you came. Dr. Stiffle and his business partner, Jeffrey Wojno, DDS, use music, art, humor, and even clothing to connect with patients, to help them overcome their fears and put them at ease. Rock songs play throughout the office at a low hum. Modern art and black-and-white photographs of musicians hang on the walls. The staff wears black T-shirts under their lab coats that feature playful, dental-meets-rock themes, such as "Plaque Sabbath," "Gums & Roses," and "For Those About to Floss, We Salute You." The T-shirt slogans were started by Dr. Stiffle but now come from patients. There are always contests for new ones, and the patients seem to wear the T-shirts as much as the staff members do, because the practice gives them away. Longtime patients aspire to collect new ones as soon as they're "issued."

As people lie down in their dental chairs, television screens above them flash pictures of patients wearing their Always There Dental Care rock 'n' roll T-shirts, smiling and waving at the camera. In one picture, a patient is wearing her T-shirt over her wedding dress. Another picture captures a patient wearing his T-shirt underwater, with a snorkel in his mouth. The photo caption is always the same: "We have the world's best patients." Dr. Stiffle takes patients' requests for songs. He makes playlists. He sings along as he bounces from chair to chair. You can hear his laughter across the office.

The informal atmosphere is all part of a strategy designed to connect with patients and exorcise fear. "We cure people of anxiety," says Dr. Stiffle. "Formality is a barrier, so we have a casual atmosphere to make patients feel good. We show you that you're not alone. We honor your anxiety and the fact that you're here in the office and made it through our door. Once you walk through it, we're going to take that anxiety away. I'm going to own it, not you," he says.

If you're guessing Dr. Stiffle must be a millennial, he's not. He's in his sixties.

Dr. Stiffle and his team reinforce the connection by making patient education a priority. The philosophy that "a healthy body begins with a healthy mouth" is emblazoned throughout the office and constantly reinforced. The staff enthusiastically uses show-and-tell models of teeth to explain the *why* behind dental procedures. "It's amazing how many people have been patients in other offices for years, and they don't know anything about the *why* behind their treatments," says Dr. Stiffle. "The consequences of not knowing the why are huge. Our view is that we're not just saving teeth; we're putting years on your life. This is why education is paramount in our office. We don't tell our patients what to do; we empower them with information so that they can make sound choices for themselves. And owning that information allows the patient to distribute it to their friends and family outside the office. It's our greatest marketing tool."

Always There Dental Care's five-star online reviews would be the envy of any small business. Behind the casual atmosphere is a practice that runs with the precision of a military operation. The staff is rigorously trained, appointments start and end on time, and the practice constantly invests in the latest technology, so much that new patients are routinely given tours of the firm's latest acquisitions. The team has mastered the art of connecting with patients through both the physical environment (place) and staff interaction (people). Like true professionals, they do it so well they make it look easy. But if it were, there might be fewer people afraid of visiting the dentist.

## MASTERING THE FUNDAMENTALS OF CONNECTION

Connecting with customers can be done any number of ways, and you should feel free to get creative, as Dr. Stiffle and his staff have done. But first, let's address some straightforward techniques and strategies that can help build a strong foundation for connection.

## Give a friendly welcome with eye contact every time.

I know what you're thinking. *Really? You have to spell this out?* I wish I didn't. It's so obvious, but I challenge you to count how many times a week you receive a friendly welcome and eye contact as a customer, whether you're at the grocery store, your local bank, or the reception desk at someone's office. Friendly greetings and eye contact are common sense, but not common practice. So often, customers are simply ignored.

Women in particular associate eye contact with listening and respect. Eye contact doesn't mean staring, of course. It's more about acknowledgment. In a world with so much choice and competition, few people need to spend a single minute (or a single dollar) with any person or business that makes them feel unwelcome or unappreciated. When you're working with couples, be sure to distribute your eye contact evenly.

From a retail standpoint, I've interviewed countless women who've told me that they've entered a store to buy something, only to leave empty-handed because they couldn't find what they were looking for and no one acknowledged or helped them. They invariably say the same three words: "I gave up."

## Be wary of opening a conversation with price.

When you meet a customer and your very first question is, "How much do you want to spend?" it can box you both into a corner before you've had the opportunity to learn about her needs.

Asking questions about needs is often the ideal starting point for conversations, and it allows you to position yourself as a resource and guide. Then the customer is likely to mention her comfort with price as you demonstrate options and ranges. *It's important to recognize that for women, the concept of value doesn't necessarily mean the lowest-priced option; it means that whatever they bought was worth more than they paid for it.* This is where service elements can play a huge role. As one research participant told me, "If something makes my life easier, I will pay for better service. For instance, if I was buying furniture, I'd ask, 'Will you haul my old sofa away? Will you help set it up?' If nothing is different, I'll go for the lower price."

## Ask icebreaker questions that invite conversation.

If you're in a retail environment and see a customer looking at a product, one way to open up a conversation is to say something like:

- "Unusual, isn't it?"
- "Interesting, isn't it?"
- "[*Insert other adjective here*], isn't it?"

Even though these are technically "closed-ended" questions, they offer a simple way to start a dialogue and connect. They can feel less intrusive to the customer because the commentary is directed at an object and not the person.

## Incorporate elements of hospitality where you can.

I recently walked into a small, independent shop in which I was asked, "Would you like a cappuccino?" It was a delicious surprise.

Yet, when you consider the proliferation of single-serve coffee machines, it's simple enough to offer. Even the shop owner's use of the word "cappuccino" instead of "coffee" conjured up an image of luxury, and also subtly communicated, "I won't be serving you coffee that's been sitting in a carafe for three hours." Most importantly, it set the tone for me to stay in the store and linger. There's no doubt: refreshments, comfortable seating, and a warm welcome are simple ways to enhance the customer experience at all kinds of business and retail environments. It's worked for human beings for thousands of years. What can you do in your own space?[2]

## Don't let your teammates sabotage your good impression.

For better or worse, your coworkers are a reflection of your company, your brand, and by extension, you. Ensure that everyone in your office or sales environment knows the importance of treating—or at a minimum, acknowledging—customers as you would, whether or not the employees are personally working with them. All staff are an important part of the cumulative impression being made, particularly for holistic buyers.

## Double down on the experience for first-time customers.

Every first-time customer is like a small miracle: out of all the things they could be doing that day, out of all the places they could be, out of all the companies they could buy from, they're buying from you. What can you do to make that first-time experience so satisfying they'll want to return again and again? Marshal your resources, for one thing. Take a cue from businesses such as high-end restaurants, where managers often create visual cues to alert staff about first-timers. These cues might be a different-colored napkin at the table, a different centerpiece, or a special order code. The idea is to make sure that every team member recognizes the first-time customer and does their best to make a positive impression. Can you do something similar with your first-timers?

## Don't just welcome—welcome back.

If you work with returning customers, using the words, "Welcome back," instead of simply, "Welcome," is a powerful form of recognition. It's human nature to want to be recognized. I once worked with a woman who went to her favorite restaurant every week for half-price wine night. She eventually stopped going because, despite making a weekly appearance for an entire year and loving the food, she was never recognized by a host or server. She couldn't take it anymore. She told me, "What is the point of being a regular if no one recognizes you?"

## "Nice to see you" is often better than "Nice to meet you."

This is especially true if you think you may have met the person before. It's a safer choice.

## Clarify name pronunciations and spelling.

If your customer is Erika with a *k* or Jazmine with a *z* or has an unusual name, you'd better believe she will notice and be impressed when you spell it and pronounce it right. Some people feel embarrassed to ask customers how to pronounce their names, and then won't use the customer's name in conversation to avoid making a mistake. This is self-defeating. When you ask for clarification, you can simply say, "I want to make sure I'm pronouncing it properly." Your customer will appreciate that you care about pronouncing it right. Clarifying name spelling is always important, even with names you feel you know well. For example, a name might be spelled Michelle or Michele. Spelling a name correctly sounds like a small detail, but if you don't do it, women may think, *If they can't get my name right, what else are they going to get wrong?* On the flip side, when you get it right, they're likely to think, *Wow, this person is really on top of things.* For women, the little things are the big things. When you get the small details right, it signals that your customers can trust you with the bigger things—like their money.

## Find an easy connection.

There's a reason so many hotel front-desk staff wear name tags emblazoned with the person's hometown or state. It's an easy point of connection with customers. "You're from Arizona? I love Arizona!" Wearing a name tag that advertises where you're from may not be appropriate for most jobs, but the idea behind finding commonality is a good one. Typically, women are looking for what they have in common with someone. If you have an office, strategically place plenty of material your customers can connect with—memorabilia, pictures of nature or family, an interesting piece of art, and so on. I interviewed one young sales professional who doesn't have kids, who reported that she keeps a photo of herself with her nieces and nephews on her desk because it gives a point of connection with customers who enjoy talking about their children and grandchildren. Keeping up with current events is another great way to make easy connections.

## Find a connection through business profiles of your customers and prospects.

In B2B sales, there's almost no excuse for not knowing something about an individual before you engage with her, if she has a business profile online. In addition to finding people and interests you may have in common, reading someone's business posts can give you an opportunity to connect in a more natural way than might not otherwise be possible. "Even something as simple as, 'I really enjoyed that article that you shared on LinkedIn; here are a few of the things I liked about it' means that suddenly you're in a conversation that has relevance to that person," says Justin Shriber, vice president of marketing for LinkedIn Sales and Marketing Solutions. Business profiles typically contain information on someone's education, career history, interests, and awards, giving you plenty of fodder with which to connect.

## "On time" means a few minutes early.

No one ever intends to be late, but we've all heard that "the road to hell is paved with good intentions." Being late by even one minute is noticeable to everyone now, since all our mobile phones are synchronized. In an ideal world, customers will never wait for you. Arriving early to appointments and meetings is one of the most important ways to demonstrate respect for someone's time. The same rule applies for conference calls. Make it your practice—if you don't already—to dial in five minutes early, and try to be the first on the line every time. Don't trip out of the starting blocks by showing up *after* your customer. Another good rule of thumb is to reconfirm how much time your customer has at the start of a call or meeting, and check in with that customer—"How are we doing on time?"—as you near the end of the time she's allotted. If you've sent someone a calendar invitation for a call from 10:00 to 10:30 a.m., it's a good idea to verbalize at 10:25 that, out of respect for her time, you'll begin wrapping up. If you need more time, ask if she's willing and able to go longer.

I'll never forget the time I mystery-shopped a mattress retailer, and the salesperson said to me, "How much time do you have to look around?" I replied that I had ten minutes. We started chatting about products and, before I knew it, she said, "According to my watch, you have three minutes left of your ten minutes. How are we doing on time?" I was blown away. I thought to myself, *This woman respects my time more than I do!* As a result, I willingly gave her more of it. Asking, "How are we doing on time?" is a technique that's especially useful for phone calls and conference calls, where you can't physically see your customer's level of engagement.

## Let customers know you're looking forward to seeing them.

People like people who like them . . . so show it! Companies in the travel industry do an excellent job of sending customers messages in advance of trips that not only remind them about their departure and arrival dates, but tell them that they're looking forward to seeing them and preparing for their arrival. It helps to drive an emotional connection, and it could be replicated any number of ways in other industries.

## Ask discovery questions with purpose.

We all know that discovery questions are meant to uncover someone's needs and qualify them. While it's important to ask such questions, you don't want your customer to feel as if she's being interrogated. A way to avoid this is to make sure every question has a purpose, so you can tell your customer why you're asking. Context is important to holistic buyers.

## Focus on the future.

When you're talking with a prospect or client, you may be firmly in the present—or, as they say in yoga class, *in the moment*—but she may be drifting off into the future as she listens to you. Even if she doesn't mention it, she's probably thinking about what buying your product will mean to her future state. Will it help her sleep better at night? Will it solve a nagging problem? Will it earn her more money, more prestige? Will she look like a hero for choosing it? Will it make her happier? Will it make the people close to her happier? Will it improve her quality of life? Save her money? She wants your product or service to do something positive for her future; otherwise, she wouldn't be buying it.

So there she is, with her mind in the future and her body in the present, either physically in front of you or at the other end of a phone/email/text or chat screen. If she's in the future, that's where you want to be too. You can travel there by painting a picture of what her life would be like if she owned your product. Think about ways to use future tense in your conversations, to help your customers visualize ownership. We'll dive more deeply into how to do this in the Lexus best practice on page 118.

## In B2B settings, give your customer a chance to speak first.

In B2B sales meetings, potential vendors are often scheduled to pitch for long stretches of time: from thirty to sixty minutes, or even longer for complex deals. After introductions and before launching into your pitch, consider taking a moment to pause and ask the clients, "Is there anything you'd like to say before we begin?" This important question may elicit new information that affects the way you position your offerings.

## Feel free to take notes.

When was the last time someone took notes when you started speaking? I bet it made an impression. I know it always does for me. While it may not be appropriate for every sales environment, taking notes shows your customer that you're actively listening and that her words are important enough to write down. This simple act serves a dual purpose, because it also allows you to record all kinds of customer details. Later, your customer will be impressed that you "remember" these details. If you have access to a good customer-relationship management (CRM) system, leverage it to the fullest.

### Find out your customer's most important priority.

Asking your customer her most important priority can help make your conversations more efficient, and, if the customer is responsive, guide you on how to serve her best. For example, I speak at a lot of conferences, and my top question for meeting planners is always, "What would make my presentation a home run for you?" Their answers provide me with an important blueprint on how to meet—and hopefully exceed—their expectations.

### If you look at a screen, it's helpful if your customers can see it too.

It's likely that most of your customers are carrying a phone on their person, perhaps visibly in front of you. Looking at screens is now a part of our common "language." If you have a customer sit at your desk while you're using a computer, try to angle the screen so she can see it too—if the information is appropriate for her to see—or risk having her turn on her own screen and focus on that instead of you.

### Turn up your empathy.

The term *mirroring* is used frequently in sales-training programs, but I believe *empathy* is the more appropriate word to describe adapting your manner to the person or people with whom you're interacting. It's a matter of paying attention to your customer's body language, eye contact, energy level, and words. When you do this, it makes it easier to approach your customer in a way that connects.

For example, if you're working with a customer who has a low-key demeanor, don't turn her off by overpowering her with personality. As an extroverted person, this is a constant challenge for me. But I've learned that if I can start at my customer's energy level, I can slowly dial it up from there.

Whether you realize it or not, your place of business has an energy level too. One funeral director I spoke with told me she's had to instruct her busy staff to never run through the funeral home as they move from one office to another, because running and looking stressed can be disruptive to grieving people who are seeking and expecting a peaceful atmosphere.

Consider the energy level of your sales environment. Customers pick up on it, and it can either help connect with them or alienate them.

## Humor can diffuse stressful situations.

Depending on the business environment, light humor can also help a customer feel better about a negative experience. I interviewed a woman named Courtney, who works in the service department of a car dealership and routinely serves customers who've had car accidents that were their own fault. When she meets customers, they are often "devastated and embarrassed," says Courtney. "I tell them, 'Welcome to the club. You aren't the first person this has happened to.' Or I'll use humor: 'The curb attacked you!' I'll make them laugh, put them at ease, tell them it happens to the best of us. I try to take the tension down a notch."

### Identify "absent influencers."

Sometimes the most important person in a sale is not the customer standing in front of you; it's the person your customer is thinking about. For example, I once interviewed a woman who was in the market for a new bed for her guest room. Even though the bed would only be used a few times a year, she was willing to pay for a quality product that would meet the criteria of her most frequent visitor: her mother. Because her mother lived in another state, she did not accompany this woman on her shopping trips for a new bed. Her mother was an "absent influencer" on the sale. This scenario is fairly common, especially with women, since they buy on behalf of so many other people. It's your job to discover who these absent influencers are, so you can address any concerns they may have and increase your chances of making the sale.

### Use politeness strategies.

Etiquette is a primary aspect of female culture, and it's something that women value in sales interactions. Women often notice when they *don't* hear politeness from sales professionals. You may find a more responsive audience when you increase polite language, for example, asking questions such as "May I?" instead of "Can I?"

### When communicating with customers, ask; don't assume.

I once had an introductory lesson with a new tennis coach, and as part of my registration process, I had to fill out my phone number on a form—*No big deal*, I thought. After my first lesson—and before I had decided to commit to more of them—I was texted frequently by the coach about all kinds of things unrelated to his programs. I found these texts intrusive, because although I had given my phone number, he had never asked permission to text me and did not identify himself, leaving me to figure out who had sent the first few messages.

When you follow up with customers, be sure to ask for their preferred method of communication. Everyone is different: some people love email, some people still like phone calls, and others only want to receive texts. Always include your name on texts, until you know you've been added to someone's contact list. There are many regulations governing text-message marketing. Make sure you're aware of the ones that are relevant to you.

## Approach "friending" with caution.

As much as you may enjoy meeting a new customer and feel as though you hit it off, think twice before friending someone with your *personal* social media accounts if she is a new customer or prospect, and you don't know her well. It's often better to stick to your professional accounts to stay connected, at least until you consider yourself to truly be friends. There are a few important reasons for this. First, you want to avoid putting your customer in an awkward position; for example, she may not want to "friend" you on Facebook and may view the request as presumptuous at best, unprofessional at worst. Then, even if she does friend you, there's a chance she might form a different opinion of you based on your personal posting history. So unless you have truly become friends with a customer, approach personal social media connections with caution. Instead, use or create separate, professional accounts exclusively for your business, which you can invite your customers to follow. You can also maintain your connections on professional networks, such as LinkedIn, which are designed expressly for that purpose.

### Don't undermine your credibility by saying phrases such as "I promise" too early.

I once walked into a store in which the sales representative greeted me by saying, "We have financing options, but I promise not to bring up money until I'm sure you're happy with your selection." I found this conversation far too premature and a little jarring because it actually *did* bring up money. Phrases like, "I promise not to bring up money," or "I promise not to sell you something you don't want," or "I promise not to overcharge you" can undermine your credibility, your pricing strategy, and the customer's trust.

### Ask customers what they hate.

If you work in an industry that offers a staggering number of product choices—like home décor or fashion accessories—it can be easier to curate options by asking your customers what styles and colors they hate instead of what they like. It's an unexpected and energizing way for customers to connect with you and begin the process of elimination. This strategy also automatically puts you on their side, as you provide reassurance for their choices. This strategy can work in almost any kind of environment. For example, if you're in B2B sales, asking your prospect what she didn't like about her last service provider can be enlightening. It also might position you as a hero because, hey, at least you aren't *those* people.

---

## Don't gossip about other customers.

This is just a reminder: don't be tempted. It only reflects poorly on you, not them. If you do this, your customers will wonder what you say about them when they're not in earshot.

## Handle multiple customers with finesse.

The inability to handle multiple customers well is a common problem in both retail and busy office settings—anywhere with low staff-to-customer ratios. How many times have you stood in front of an employee who ignored you while you patiently waited for him or her to deal with someone else, without the person even looking up to acknowledge your existence? This kind of behavior can make customers' blood boil. Most of the time, people will have patience as long as they're briefly acknowledged with eye contact and an upheld index finger that suggests the person will be with them shortly, or a whispered, "I'll be with you in just a moment." Basic acknowledgment is the simple solution.

## Be kid and companion friendly.

Your customer may be shopping with other people, such as children, who are unenthusiastic about being in your place of business. Make her life easier by welcoming and accommodating her companions, so she can complete her mission. Though this goal can be accomplished in many creative ways, one simple solution is to place chairs in your sales or retail environment.[3] Since smartphones have eradicated boredom as we know it, sometimes all people need is a place to sit down and use their devices. This is smart business: few things can stop a woman's shopping trip faster than bored or cranky companions.

### Remember: clothes don't make the customer.

Many women tell me they feel profiled based on their dress when they interact with salespeople—and not in a good way. There's a famous scene in the 1990 movie *Pretty Woman*, starring Julia Roberts and Richard Gere, in which salespeople at a boutique on Beverly Hills' Rodeo Drive refuse to help Roberts's character because of the way she is dressed (they think she looks "cheap"). They don't realize she has serious money to spend. Ultimately, her character drops loads of money at other stores, then goes back to the place where the salespeople ignored her. "Do you remember me?" she asks. "I was in here yesterday. You wouldn't wait on me?" Then, lifting her huge shopping bags, she says, "Big mistake. Big. Huge!"[4] Given that we live in an extravagantly casual society, where black yoga pants can be paired with a jacket and classified as formal attire (I've done it myself), it's an understatement to say that judging your customers on what they're wearing can result in missed opportunities. As they say in the movies: Big mistake. Big. Huge. I once interviewed a woman who felt that she was negatively profiled for her casual clothes. She said, "I wanted to scream, 'I have two master's degrees!'"

### Use the boomerang strategy to avoid TMPI: too much personal information.

When you find great points of connection with customers, it's important to avoid going down a rabbit hole of talking too much about your own experiences instead of your customers'. The reality is that, unless you're already friends, customers often won't be interested in your personal experiences unless they're relevant to the product or service you're selling. Many a sale has been killed through a salesperson sharing TMPI—*too much personal information*. Self-awareness is critical here. I've been on the receiving end of salespeople sharing experiences that range from their digestive problems to bunion pain, with the occasional *let me show you my scar* thrown in. These people were perfect strangers.

That, of course, is not you. But it's easy to go down a rabbit hole of personal stories, even with benign topics. The smart strategy is to say just enough about yourself to establish something in common with the customer, or to emphasize why you are the most knowledgeable person for her to work with, *and then not dwell on it*. I recommend what I call the "boomerang strategy." This is a technique in which you acknowledge what you and the customer have in common and then throw the conversation right back at the customer so she can keep telling her story. Here's how it works:

Customer: I just got back from Disney World.

Sales professional: You're kidding! I just went to Disney World a few months ago! Wasn't it fantastic? I loved it. What was your favorite ride?

Customer: My kids really liked Space Mountain. In fact, the line was really long, but then we saw . . .

At this point, the topic has been safely boomeranged back to the customer. Remember this strategy throughout the course of customer conversations, and keep throwing that boomerang right back. You will be viewed as a great conversationalist.

An important exception to this rule is when you have personal experience with the product or service she's interested in. In these situations, share your experiences and firsthand perspective. It's a great way to make a connection.

## Leverage team selling for awkward situations.

Through no fault of our own, we may often find ourselves working with a customer with whom we just don't connect. In these situations, don't hesitate to bring in a teammate to help you work with the customer to make the experience better for everyone.

## Avoid "friendly fire."

Don't talk badly about your coworkers, your management, or your job. From the customers' perspective, it reflects poorly on you and can undermine your credibility.

## BEST PRACTICE

## Innovative Office Solutions
*Creating an Emotional Connection in a Commoditized Business*

Selling both paper clips and high-level business strategy to the same clients is a triumph of customer connection. It's all in a day's work for Jennifer Smith, CEO of Innovative Office Solutions, the largest women-owned, independent business-products dealer in the country. Headquartered in Minnesota, this $130 million office supply and furniture company is thriving in a famously price-driven, commoditized business that has long served women as buyers and decision makers. The company's guiding principle is "Relationships Matter," and its customer retention rate is in the 90 percent range. How it's achieved this rate is instructive for anyone looking to deepen his or her connections with customers.

Innovative sells every kind of product you would ever need for an office space, from the bathroom soap to the desks. The office products business has been greatly impacted by the digital world. "People are using less paper, file folders, filing cabinets, staplers, and toner," says Smith. "We've had to reinvent ourselves to stay relevant." Finding new avenues for growth and earning the loyalty of customers who could easily buy from big-box competitors has been a priority. The company has succeeded by implementing strategies centered on customer connection. Let's look at three of them.

1. *Offering solutions, not just products.* The most foundational strategy for Innovative was expanding the company's offerings beyond transactional products, such as pens and toilet paper, into more emotionally engaging territory, like corporate culture consulting and workspace design. "Our industry is totally commoditized, and we knew we had to take it to the next level by offering solutions and not just products," says Smith. Innovative added office furniture, interior design, and corporate branding capabilities, which opened the door for its sales team to talk with customers on topics such as corporate culture and talent

recruitment. When the conversations expanded, so did the customers. Innovative moved from selling primarily to administrative staff to C-suite executives, because a company's office environment and culture are important aspects in the war for talent. "When you can help a company bring their corporate culture to life, that takes the customer relationship to a different level," says Smith. Innovative's ability to help clients with corporate-culture strategy is remarkable when you consider the firm also sells toilet paper to those very same customers.

2. *Creating relationship-management teams.* "The number one pain point for customers in our industry is reaching out to call centers and talking to someone who doesn't know them," says Smith, "and then dealing with a different person for every product group they buy." To solve this pain point, Innovative created relationship-management teams, called studios, that are dedicated to each customer and provide support across product categories. "Not only does this make things easier for our customers, it allows us to sell on the basis of simplifying their supply chain and reducing their soft costs, because they can move from having seven different vendors to just one."

3. *Empowering employees to solve customer issues.* A third strategy was to implement a program that enables every person at the company to fix a customer problem on the spot, called "Make It Right." "Whether it's a driver or an accounting person, if a customer is not happy, every employee is empowered to fix a situation immediately to make it right, without waiting for approval from someone else." The company holds monthly internal events in which everyone who's had a "Make It Right"

moment shares their story to help their colleagues prevent future mistakes. "In the beginning, no one wanted to admit they'd done something wrong," says Smith. "It took us a long time to create a culture in which people look at the experience through a different lens, in terms of owning the customer relationship, doing whatever they need to do to make things right, and then paying it forward by talking about it in front of their colleagues. That's where our own corporate culture comes in. If your whole team is on the same page and they know what their purpose is and how they contribute, your customers can sense it and they think, *I want to work with this company*."

Innovative's success shows the power of staying laser-focused on customer connection. Smith believes the company's strong customer relationships will sustain them through future disruptions. "Now, even office furniture is commoditizing, so it all comes back to having amazing relationships with your clients so that they trust you and want to buy anything that you come out with."

## KEY TAKEAWAYS

- There is no end to the creativity you can use to deepen your customer connections. Dr. Stiffle uses rock 'n' roll, patient education, and an informal atmosphere, which are reflections of his personality and interests. Innovative Office

Solutions expanded its product offerings with emotionally engaging solutions like corporate-culture strategy.
- Connecting with women buyers at an interpersonal level means finding common ground, avoiding outdated stereotypes, and demonstrating that you're actively listening through words and eye contact.

## ACTIVATING YOUR INSIGHTS

- Imagine that someone felt so strongly connected to your business that she wanted to get a tattoo of your logo. (Work with me here—it's a brainstorm! And don't forget, people already do this with brands such as Harley-Davidson and Nike.) What are the kinds of things you could do to generate that kind of loyalty and connection? Create a list of ideas, and pick the top one or two to execute.
- What are the three top ways that you connect with customers currently? How can you expand on these efforts to create even deeper connections?

## CHAPTER 5

# MOTIVATOR #2: INSPIRED

## Inspire Your Customers to Do Business with You

People will tell you they don't like to be "sold," but the truth is that we love to buy from people who inspire us with passion and knowledge about their products. In those moments, it doesn't feel as though we're being sold; it feels like we're being helped, and that our lives are improving in some way through the experience. Inspiration can happen in the most unexpected ways, in the unlikeliest of businesses: even rodent control. Yes, rodent control. Let me tell you, if someone who extinguishes mice for a living can deliver an inspiring customer experience, anybody can. I've witnessed it, and here's how it happened.

There were five houses under construction on my city block in Chicago. One day, our neighborhood newsletter sent out an alert that, due to all the construction, unwelcome vermin (the kind with beady eyes and tails) were on the loose in the neighborhood. I felt compelled to call a pest-control company to protect our home from invasion. I had never bought this type of service before and chose the company based solely on their online reviews.

On the morning of my appointment, the doorbell rang, and I opened it to see a tall man sporting a bushy beard, mirrored sunglasses, and impressive tattoos. He introduced himself and handed me his business card. He then asked permission to enter my home, which struck me as being exceptionally polite. As we sat in the living room, he asked me what had prompted my call to the company and listened quietly—without interrupting me—while I explained the situation. He then asked what I knew about rodents. My answer was, "Zero." He nodded and asked if I'd like to know a little bit more about mice and rats in an urban habitat and what he could do to prevent them from setting foot in my home. I was intrigued and said yes. Then he gave me a brief master class on rodent life and death, the likes of which I had never heard.

I will spare you the fascinating details, but what struck me most was how he talked about his company's solution. He began by saying, "Here's what's different about how we approach the problem versus our competitors," and went on to articulate what he viewed as their superior extermination process. I was mesmerized. He was clearly proud of his work. Never in my life had I met someone as passionate or as knowledgeable about rodent control.

We all know this is an easy industry to ridicule. Yet, this man didn't make fun of his job. He didn't make sarcastic remarks about life in the rodent-control business. He delivered the information with the seriousness of a man on a mission, and that mission was to protect my home. Elevating his offering as "home protection" and not just "pest control" increased my emotional engagement. Before our meeting, I was only in the market for the bare minimum solution. By the end of our conversation, I bought everything he was selling. And I'm happy to say that, as of this writing, the only mammals living in my house are the ones that are supposed to be there.

Most of us would be hard-pressed to think of a less appealing service to sell—or buy—than pest control. And yet I had a great, and even inspiring, experience with this company. When the salesperson left my house, I felt smarter than I had when I woke up that morning; I learned about a subject I had previously known nothing about; I found a solution to a potential problem; I discovered a service provider I felt I could trust; and, consequently, I felt great about the money I was spending and with whom I was spending it. My experience offers a great example of the fact that, in sales, enthusiasm is contagious. When you're passionate about what you do, people respond, no matter what you're selling.

When women have a great experience with a sales professional, they almost always describe it to me this way: "That person wasn't trying to sell me; they were trying to *help* me." That's what an inspirational sales experience feels like: it's so helpful it lifts the customer to a level of satisfaction she never expected.

## MASTERING THE FUNDAMENTALS OF INSPIRATION

Here's an easy way to think about inspiration: What can you say or do that would get your customer to utter the word *wow*? We'll go over some ideas to get you started, including best practices from companies as disparate as a bike retailer in California and a global plumbing manufacturer, but first let's cover some of the basics for inspiring your customers.

## Don't just sell—educate.

Make it your goal to have your customers feel more enlightened just for doing business with you. Show that you're invested in their knowledge, and it will have an impact. When appropriate, educate customers on your industry or category and not just your product, as my pest-control expert did, and as the dentist Dr. Stiffle does. Remember that no matter what product or service you represent, you're really selling only one thing, and that's help.[1]

## Know your company's history, mission, and values.

If someone has never done business with your firm, help create an emotional connection by describing your company's history, mission, values, and unique point of view. You already know that customers want to feel good about the people and companies they buy from, and this is particularly true with women, as well as with younger customers of both genders.

## Curate options by talking about what's popular or bestselling.

It's human nature to be interested in what other people are buying, which is just one reason e-commerce businesses almost always feature "best sellers" as a category. Talking about what's popular with other customers is a great anchoring technique that helps customers zero in on a focused number of options. It also provides reassurance, because there's safety in numbers. No matter how you do it, find a way to flag what's popular and bestselling before your customer has to ask.

## Point out invisible product attributes to underscore value.

Chances are, your customer can't physically see every valuable attribute that's built into your product or service. Think of invisible materials in consumer products, such as Scotchgard fabric protector, polarized lenses, performance materials, and weatherproofing, to name just a handful. Don't assume your customer already knows about these attributes; point them out to underscore the value she'll be getting for the price. And when you do, focus on the talk-worthy details that people will want to share with others. Imagine a home builder saying, "The ceilings in this home are a foot higher than the ones you'll see from other builders, and that's what makes the space feel larger." It's easy to imagine a customer repeating those exact words as she shows her friends her new home.

## Engage the senses; women shop with all of them.

Women are highly attuned to detail and ambiance, from scent to lighting to music, to the tactile nature of touching and examining products. I often hear women identify stores like Anthropologie, Trader Joe's, and IKEA as favorite places to shop, because of the high sensory engagement within them. My local grocery store, Mariano's, features a live pianist playing a grand piano near the checkout line on weekends, which creates an enjoyable atmosphere for all the people waiting in long lines. When evaluating your business, determine how many senses are being engaged within your own four walls. Can you add even one more?

## Give hands-on demonstrations.

You don't want your customers to be passive observers in the sales process. Whenever it's appropriate, invite them to touch and feel the products you're selling. Hands-on demonstrations are also effective for conversations about materials and invisible product qualities, for example, "Feel the weight of this wood," or "Feel the lightness in these titanium frames." Is there a natural way for you to use the hands-on technique in your work?

## Create inspiring names for your products.

Clever names add interest and personality to even the most basic products and services. Nail polish brands mastered this long ago: OPI's "I'm Not Really a Waitress" and Essie's "Ballet Slippers" are legendary. If your products don't have inspiring names, give them some. Look to the apparel industry for good examples. Former indie retailer ModCloth—now owned by Walmart—has a habit of giving their products arresting names like "Biking through Brussels A-Line Dress," "Star of the Seminar Top," and "Pontoon Cruise One-Piece Swimsuit." The company's cofounder, Susan Koger, once told me in an interview, "We view the clothing as content and not just merchandise."[2] This strategy can apply to any kind of business. When done well, product naming ignites the imagination and allows you to tell a story. How can you leverage this strategy to inspire your own customers?

## Create experiences that drive emotional engagement.

Sports apparel retailers like lululemon and Athleta offer in-store yoga and fitness classes; Home Depot offers do-it-yourself workshops for kids and adults; Williams-Sonoma offers cooking classes. What activities can you add to complement the products and services that you sell? To stoke your own inspiration, look outside your industry and make field trips to businesses that routinely deliver experiences, such as Eataly and American Girl. If you're in B2B sales, what seminars or experiences can you create?

## Tell happy customer stories.

Telling stories about happy customers adds third-party credibility to sales conversations and, often, an effective dash of inspiration. People love hearing about what's worked for others; for example, "We have several customers who turned their guest room into a home office with this furniture. One of them told us she loves it so much she started a new business working from home." Amass your best customer stories and have them at the ready to use in customer conversations. They're so important that they might be what your customers remember most about their conversations with you. These stories also give you a valuable opportunity to demonstrate how your knowledge made the difference for someone.

## Encourage reviews.

Encourage your customers to write reviews. This sounds like an obvious strategy, but I've met many sales professionals who are self-conscious about asking for them. This is understandable, but for better or worse, we live in an age in which reviews and customer testimonials are crucial for attracting new customers. Many people include hyperlinks to review sites with their requests, to make it easier for customers. Feature the best reviews prominently on your website and marketing materials, provided you have your customers' permission to do so. If you're on LinkedIn, you can ask customers to write recommendations directly on your profile page. There's no end to the variety of ways businesses are now asking for and collecting reviews. At my local hair salon, for example, customers are encouraged to post a review of their haircut while they're still in the salon, and when they do, they receive a discount on the cut. Just be sure to develop a reviews policy that aligns with state, country, and website legal requirements.

## Demonstrate how your business makes the world a better place.

People want their purchases to have meaning, and this is especially true with women buyers. If you haven't already articulated this, begin by asking yourself this question: "When my customer buys from me, what does it say about her?" Consider the appeal of TOMS, the company that created the "Exhibit A" of big, inspirational business ideas.[3] TOMS donates one pair of shoes to a needy child for every pair purchased by a customer and has a similar program for its eyewear line, its coffee line (it donates water), and its bag line (it donates birth kits and funding for skilled birth attendants). Target offers a different example with its long history of partnering with top fashion designers to offer exclusive-yet-affordable apparel and accessories. Many independent retailers display signs that encourage customers to "Shop Small," "Buy Independent," or "Support your Neighborhood Businesses," and emphasize their role in keeping the community vibrant. How does what you offer make the world a better place in some small (or big) way? If you're doing great things, let people know it. Don't take it for granted that they do. It could tip the balance in whether someone chooses to buy from you or someone else.

## Think visually, and invest in design.

Good design is inspiring, and it's now become a decision-making factor for women in categories far outside fashion and apparel. You see it in the smallest of products, like cans of LaCroix water, all the way to the largest, like Tesla cars. My Kleenex box looks like something out of *Architectural Digest*. My orange Poppin stapler is positively chic.[4]

Of course, design isn't just about how something looks; it's also about how well something works. This is why service businesses aren't off the hook when it comes to design. Whether it's your website, your retail location, your call center experience, or your app, people expect customer interfaces to be intuitive and even elegant. Call it the Apple effect or the Target effect; the bottom line is that design can no longer be viewed as separate and distinct from marketing and sales functions. They are joined at the hip. Well-designed products and experiences can help you command higher price points. How can you elevate design within your own product or service?[5]

## Offer complete solutions.

Women's holistic buying style is an opportunity for you to bundle products that go together. Let's say you're working in a store and meet a customer looking at a new lamp for her living room. As she contemplates buying it, she may be thinking about how that lamp is going to change the entire look of the room. She starts thinking that she may need a new rug, a new chair, or even a new paint job to complete the look. This is big-picture thinking in action. In your own business, think about ways that you can package and price products that naturally go with one another. Don't always leave it to your customers to piece things together. Even if they don't want a package you're featuring, just the idea of a package may inspire them to piece together their own. Taking it one step further, is it possible for customers to build a collection of what you sell?

## Focus on real-life benefits.

Product specs and industry jargon can weigh down a sales conversation. If you work in an industry filled with jargon, challenge yourself to minimize the jargon and name at least one real-life benefit for every feature you mention. You can also create helpful analogies as descriptions. For example, in the eyewear industry, polarized lenses command a premium, but not everyone knows what "polarized" means. A great analogy that I've heard from sales professionals in the industry is that polarized lenses "are like sunscreen for your eyes." What analogies can you come up with for your own products?

## Emphasize how the people in your customers' lives will benefit and react positively to their product choice.

We humans are wired to avoid social rejection. Once you've used discovery questions to identify your customers' absent influencers—the people who aren't present but are critical to the sale—be sure to emphasize how they, too, will benefit from what you're selling.

## Tell the backstory.

It's likely that some of your products and services have interesting backstories. Maybe your firm created a new product based on customer feedback; maybe your designer built something inspired by a hike up Mount Everest; maybe you are the only firm in the country with an exclusive on a particular material. Let your customers know the backstory behind your products, services, and designs. It gives you great material with which to engage them in conversation. Look to IKEA for inspiration here: the company routinely showcases photos and stories of its product designers inside the company's stores.

## Elevate the ordinary; consider your signs.

The way you merchandise your space can render whatever you're selling more valuable. This is why many people stage houses with great furniture and art before putting them up for sale; they hope it will help command a higher price for the home. If you think of your selling environment as a stage, consider your signage and decor to be your supporting cast.

From a retail perspective, signs are often a missed opportunity for selling and brand building. Sure, signs are everywhere, but mostly they're directional or informational. I once saw a great example of inspirational signage at Lowe's, a chain of big-box home improvement stores, and it left a strong impression on me. I was walking down an aisle that featured some low-interest (to me) products, like baskets full of loose cabinet knobs. As I walked past the knobs, I looked up and saw a banner promoting them, which read, "Cabinet and Pantry Solutions: Turn Chaos into Calm." It gave me pause. The banner conveyed an emotional benefit for all those functional cabinet knobs.

Then I moved farther down the aisle and found sets of plastic dish-drying racks for sale. *Boring stuff*, I thought, until I looked up and another banner beckoned. It read, "Countertop and Sink Solutions: Turn Boring into Beautiful." I considered the message and thought to myself, *Yes, if your kitchen is sparkling clean, I guess it really is a beautiful thing.*

Finally, I turned the corner and saw displays of the most dull products imaginable: plastic silverware holders that live inside kitchen drawers and eventually get filled with crumbs. I looked up, and the banner read, "Drawer Solutions: Turn Scattered into Streamlined." It was yet another emotionally engaging message. I was impressed: Lowe's had elevated ordinary products to an inspirational place. If Lowe's can do it with cabinet knobs and plastic silverware holders, imagine what you can do with your own products.

## Assess your communication materials.

Since we're talking about signs, now might be a good time to take an inventory of your communications materials to determine if they are inspiring, inclusive, and relevant to modern women. Use these tips as your guide on mistakes to avoid.[6]

*Mistake #1: Overplaying feminine stereotypes.* Generally speaking, don't use a heavy hand with pink for selling to women unless you're in the fashion and beauty businesses, or raising money for breast cancer causes. There are exceptions of course, but in gender-neutral industries, an excessive use of pink—and exclusively pink—can come across as a cliché when targeting women. Ideally, if pink is used, it should be used as one color among many. Cautiously approach other stereotypical images for women, such as red stilettos, purses, and lipstick marks, unless you're selling those products.

*Mistake #2: Using outdated language.* The word *women* usually sounds more modern than *ladies*, especially if you are in a business that's new to reaching out to women. Keep in mind that language changes over time; for example, the word *stewardess* has evolved to *flight attendant*. Make it a priority to stay current. Also be wary of using the word *females* to refer to groups of women, because the plural term can seem impersonal. Try the word *women* instead.

*Mistake #3: Depicting women as passive observers.* Closely examine the photographs you use, to make sure they're not dominated by images of women in passive poses. Men are depicted as "agents of action" in marketing more often than women. Images of women who merely gaze at other people doing things are out of touch with the reality of modern women's lives. Use an "active" lens as you evaluate stock photography for websites and presentations, and buy the best quality you can afford.

*Mistake #4: Leaving women out of the picture entirely.* One lingering mistake for many industries, even today, is leaving women out of visuals entirely. Recently, I was at an airport rental car facility that was filled with women customers standing in line for service, yet every poster in the building showcased men—and only men—renting cars. Watch your blind spot and ensure that women are represented in your visuals.

## Folsom Bike

*Making Inspiration Look as Easy as Riding a Bike*

If you're in the business of selling bikes, you want as many people as possible to get cycling. Yet walking into a bike shop can be an intimidating experience for the uninitiated. That's the very reason Erin Gorrell and her husband Wilson Gorrell opened their own bicycle retailing business in Folsom, California. Today, if you hang out at one of their two bike shops long enough, it's clear that the Gorrells aren't just selling bikes—they're selling inspiration. And they're good at it: Folsom Bike is now the largest locally owned bike retailer in bicycle-crazy Northern California. Looking at the way they've grown their business offers valuable lessons in customer inspiration. Erin Gorrell tells us their story:

"When I wrote our business plan, I felt that customer service was really lacking in this industry, and as a woman cyclist visiting bike shops around the country, I saw how often the treatment of women was even worse. So when I opened our store, I wanted to have a hospitality approach. I wanted to be the Nordstrom of bike shops. I wanted to be like *Cheers*,[7] where everybody knows your name."

To create this kind of environment, the Gorrells built a café in one of their stores, called Folsom Grind, whose motto is "Get grind in your cup before you grind on your bike." It's become the heart of the Folsom Bike community and a place to get introduced to fellow cyclists and potential friends. "Any type of sport becomes very much a community thing, and cycling falls into that realm," says Gorrell. "Our goal was that if you lived in the area and wanted to bike, you knew to come to us. The coffee shop was our vehicle to make that happen, and it's been extremely successful." Gorrell says she wanted to give people a nonthreatening reason to come to the store. "What could be more nonthreatening than a cup of coffee? It doesn't cost you a whole lot of money. People drink it every morning. So we dedicated twelve hundred square feet of interior space and a large outdoor patio to it."

Gorrell reports that the café is routinely filled with customers, riding groups, friends, and "civilians" who gather there before and after rides to hang out and drink coffee, local beer, and wine, and often talk about their latest rides. The Gorrells intentionally built an environment in which people want to linger and chat, both in the café and inside the stores. There's seating everywhere. "We have bar stools in front of the service counter in the stores; we have sofas; we have chairs—we want our customers to interact with staff and just hang out with us," says Gorrell. "We want to get to know them, and we want them to get to know us, because that's what builds customers for life." The staff is constantly curating group rides for different ages, interests, and fitness levels, as well as offering training seminars, inviting guest speakers, and hosting events like the annual Women, Wine & Dirt mountain bike ride. "We're constantly planting mustard seeds (of inspiration)," she says.

"The whole focus of our business is showing our customer 'this could be you,'" says Gorrell. "This could be you on that mountain. This could be you on that road. This could be you buying a new bike. It's about how we make people feel. That's what they remember. And we want to make people feel good."

Folsom Bike also has a mission to inspire and cater to women. The Gorrells built a store-within-a-store Ride Like a Girl boutique that features T-shirts, water bottles, and merchandise emblazoned with that slogan, which was created by Erin Gorrell. "The response has been phenomenal," she says. "Women are so appreciative and thankful that they don't have to hunt and peck to find something that fits them. Cycling has been predominantly a male sport. As a woman, you don't want to be made to feel inadequate when you walk into a store. You want to be enlightened, educated, and excited. That's what we provide."

## Inspiring Customers Helps Prevent Showrooming

For brick-and-mortar businesses, giving inspiring service is critical to curbing showrooming, the practice of visiting a store to look at merchandise and then buying it cheaper online. Erin Gorrell frequently meets customers who have found cheaper bikes online, but she knows how to inspire them and earn their business with personalized service.

"You can't ride a bike on the internet," says Gorrell. "The internet can't know what your goals are. We can find out your goals through active listening. Let's say you're looking at a bike online, and you want to go downhill riding in Lake Tahoe. You may be looking at a bike that won't be able to do that. We are going to make sure you're on the right bike, that the right parts are installed, and that your bike is shifting 100 percent correctly. And then we're going to have you ride it, so you can feel what the brakes are like. You can throw your leg over it. We're going to send you across the street on a bike path, and we're going to make you ride a hill on three or four different bikes, so that you can make the best, informed decision. Give us the opportunity to match the price you see online, and we will deliver your bike to you. We show the value to the customer and then add an additional layer of complimentary services (like delivery) to show that we exceed what the internet can do."

## Beware of These Inspiration Killers

Folsom Bike has a customer experience centered on inspiration. Based on my research with women, inspirational sales experiences are the exceptions and not the rule. To deliver an inspiring experience, be sure to avoid these inspiration killers:

- Demonstrating a lack of interest in what you're selling
- Avoiding eye contact
- Using sarcasm or complaining when referring to your job or product
- Diverting attention from the customer to yourself
- Appearing distracted by looking at your phone (if you're on the phone doing something for the customer, explain this to them)
- Producing work with simple mistakes, like spelling errors
- Showing up late

**BEST PRACTICE**

# Kohler Co.
### *Inspiration in Everything, Including the Kitchen Sink*

If you're renovating a bathroom and shopping for a new sink, what's more inspiring to see at stores: rows of sinks bolted onto walls, or sinks that are situated in beautiful bathroom displays?

The displays, of course, but they're not always easy to find in retail environments, since they take up valuable square footage. This poses a challenge for plumbing brands, because there's not always room to showcase how products such as showerheads, toilets, faucets, and cast-iron tubs can create a look in someone's home. To overcome this, global manufacturing giant Kohler Co. broke out of plumbing-industry norms and created its own line of direct-to-consumer stores, to inspire customers to build their dream homes with Kohler products. The company's rollout of two retail concepts, Kohler Signature Stores and Kohler Experience Centers, offer great lessons for any business looking to bring its brand to life within four walls.

## Dream. Design. Shop.

Walking into a Kohler Signature Store is like stepping into every fantasy you've ever had about rehabbing your home. The space is filled with beautiful bathroom and kitchen vignettes in every conceivable style and color palette, complete with elements such as wood cabinetry, tiles, modern lighting, and accessories so detailed that even the soap dishes look like works of art.

"We reverse engineered the stores based on what the customer wanted, and our customer base is 80 percent female," says Michelle Kilmer, Kohler director of stores and showroom marketing. "Our message is focused on three things: dream, design, shop," she explains. "We also offer professional design services and connect our customers with installation experts, because we wanted to put control in the hands of the customer."

At the Kohler Experience Centers, which are expanded, premium versions of the Signature Stores, displays are so sophisticated that customers can see and feel running water from products like rain showers, handheld spray wands, and faucets. They can even bring a bathing suit to take a private test shower in one of the stores' spa-like "experience rooms." Yes, you can now test-drive a shower, which gives new meaning to the idea of an immersive brand experience.

You probably didn't grow up visiting "plumbing stores" because the industry historically is a wholesale business. Kohler started to change that in 2005, a year when the US economy was going gangbusters, HGTV was becoming wildly popular, and interior design was moving beyond the *Architectural Digest* crowd and into the mass market. Suddenly, people felt empowered to create their own dream bathrooms and kitchens.

Enter Kohler, which became the first plumbing manufacturer to launch a direct-to-consumer retail strategy in the form of Kohler Signature Stores. Prior to the launch of these stores, customers had fewer places to see the kinds of luxury bathroom and kitchen designs featured in Kohler's stylized advertising campaigns. Websites such as Houzz and Pinterest hadn't been invented yet. Unless someone visited a plumbing showroom or hired a professional interior designer, it wasn't always easy to see Kohler products *in situ*, and thus the manufacturer was missing out on the opportunity to inspire retail shoppers and help them imagine how the products could transform their homes.

By creating a direct-to-consumer retail channel of its own, Kohler was able to showcase the variety of designs, price points, and footprints available from the company all under one roof for the first time, while maintaining a high level of customer service to match the inspirational environment. Service is important because of the high-stakes decision-making involved in home building and rehab. Customers are well aware that they may have to live with their choices for decades, and no one wants to make mistakes. Kohler Signature Stores became the first in the plumbing industry to offer fee-based, professional design expertise at retail. As a result, the stores evolved into inspirational one-stop shops for kitchen and bathroom renovations for retail customers.

The stores serve a B2B role for the company as well. Kohler trade channel partners—plumbers, contractors, architects, and interior designers—bring their clients to the stores to see all the Kohler possibilities for their projects in one place. Each store is operated by a local plumbing distributor through a licensing agreement, which means that when customers buy from a Kohler store, they are supporting a local business while getting a global brand, offering both the appeal of shopping local and the peace of mind of purchasing a known product.

What's next for Kohler? The company plans to continue rolling out new stores. It now has more than thirty stores in the

Americas and more than nine hundred branded stores in China. The manufacturer also has introduced online (virtual) bathroom design services. "Our goal is to meet the customer wherever they are," says Kilmer.

---

## KEY TAKEAWAYS

- You can inspire customers by what you do (your product), how you do it (your service), where you do it (your physical space), why you do it (your mission and values), and who you are (your unique personality and style). Kohler and Folsom Bike offer compelling examples of the different ways that inspiration can be brought to life.
- Your ability to inspire customers can lead them to value your guidance, overcome price concerns, and choose you over a competitor. My rodent-control sales professional was effective in inspiring my high-dollar purchase by elevating his offerings from pest control to home protection, which inspired me to follow his advice.

## ACTIVATING YOUR INSIGHTS

- Your best customer stories can inspire prospects and new customers. With that in mind, consider creating a

"Happy Customer Story Repository." This repository is a compilation of your best and most inspiring customer stories, documented in a file so that they're top of mind and can be referenced in future customer conversations. If you work with a team, collaborate on the repository so you can share each other's customer stories and have that many more to tell.

- Think about all the things you do for customers that might cause them to say, "Wow!" What are some ways you can create more "wow" moments, like the test showers at Kohler Experience Centers and the test rides at Folsom Bike? Can you expand on the "wow" moments you already offer?

- Ultimately, people are inspired to buy something when they feel it will improve their lives. How can you more effectively articulate how much better someone's life will be if they buy your product or service?

## CHAPTER 6

# MOTIVATOR #3: CONFIDENT

*Instill Customers' Confidence in You and Your Products*

At the most high-profile speaking engagement of my career, I had the kind of confidence crisis most male speakers never have to worry about. I was in Las Vegas, and an hour before my presentation, I was led backstage to meet a makeup artist who'd been assigned to make all the speakers look fabulous for their big moment onstage. As I sat in a chair, the artist began applying makeup, and I quickly realized there was no mirror for me to watch what was happening: we were in a windowless room with bare walls. I sat for forty-five minutes while she put on what felt like thousands of products.

Normally, I don't wear much makeup, and I became increasingly uncomfortable as my presentation time drew nearer. *What is she doing to me?* I thought.

When she finally finished, I stood up and walked over to a mirror on the other side of the room for the "reveal." I didn't recognize myself. There was more makeup on my face than I'd ever worn in my life. Bright red lipstick, thick black eyeliner . . . the look screamed "Las Vegas showgirl" instead of "competent business executive." The next ten minutes were spent in a panic as I asked the makeup artist to scrape everything off my face before I walked onstage. I was rattled by the experience. Instead of bolstering my confidence, the makeover had shaken it. I thought to myself, *I bet this never happens at Sephora.*

Why did Sephora come to mind in that moment? Because feeling confident with beauty products is something I associate with that brand. I'm not alone. Owned by French luxury group LVMH, Sephora has more than twenty-five hundred stores in thirty-four countries and is the number one specialty beauty retailer in the world.[1] It got there by building customer confidence in both the products it sells and the experience it delivers.

## BEST PRACTICE

### Sephora
*Confidence Is Beautiful*

The entire beauty industry is built on selling confidence. My nightmare makeover in Las Vegas could have been someone else's dream look, but it sure wasn't mine. How does any retailer drive customer confidence in an industry that's so wildly subjective? Sephora has the key, and its innovative strategies provide valuable insights for any brand. Because no matter what product or service you represent, confidence closes sales.

Sephora sales associates—the company calls them beauty advisors—help customers feel confident about their product choices through a blend of technology and "analog" customer experiences. "Our stores are a stage, and our beauty advisors provide performance and real interaction with our clients, not just transactions," says Mary Beth Laughton, Sephora executive vice president of omni retail for the US market. "We use technology to complement the beauty advisors' expertise . . . and to make them even more powerful."

Sephora stores carry more than two hundred brands, and beauty advisors must cater to the full spectrum of customer needs, from self-service product replenishment ("I'm out of my favorite lipstick and need a new one") to beauty transformations ("I'm ready for a whole new look") to playful experimentation ("I want to try one of those glowing highlighters"). They do it using tools the company has built to help with different customer paths. These tools help beauty advisors curate the brand's vast number of products in a way that makes customers feel more certain they're buying the right ones for their needs.

Every industry has customer pain points, and in beauty, one issue rises above the rest: finding products that perfectly match someone's skin tone. This is especially difficult with foundation, the product serving as the makeup "base," which is applied to the face before anything else. The number of choices is overwhelming: Sephora alone offers more than 130 different foundation collections and 3,000 different shades. Women can tell you that it's easy to buy the wrong shade of foundation because it might look great under a store's fluorescent lights, but terrible under different lighting. To solve this pain point and help customers feel confident about their choice, Sephora partnered with Pantone, the company best known for its color-matching system, to create a tool called Color iQ.

Here's how it works: a Sephora beauty advisor holds up a handheld device, about the size of a phone, to a customer's face, capturing several different images of her skin. Once the images are captured, the digital tool assigns the customer a Color iQ number. Armed with her personalized Color iQ number, the customer can identify all the products that will match her skin tone across every brand Sephora carries. The technology has taken the concept of product curation to a whole new level and has been expanded to include additional product categories such as skincare and even fragrance.

Another area of the business that's designed to drive customer confidence is the beauty makeover, a staple of the industry. Nobody wants a customer to walk away unhappy from a makeover, as I did in Las Vegas, because if she doesn't feel great about the way she looks, there's little chance she'll buy the products that were used on her. To increase customers' confidence, Sephora created an augmented reality tool called Sephora Virtual Artist, which lets customers see photos of themselves "wearing" different makeup looks and products. Beauty advisors use this tool to allow customers to choose their favorite look before the makeover begins. "It helps Beauty Advisors talk to clients about what they're aiming for in advance," says Laughton. "There's this meeting of the minds . . . and it increases the client's confidence." This tool is also available directly to consumers through the Sephora website and app, allowing people to "try on" different looks and makeup colors at home, with augmented reality.

Sephora also has transformed the classic makeover experience into an opportunity to collect customer data. Beauty advisors scan information on the products applied during a makeover, and at the end of the session they send that information to the customer so she can buy the products and replicate the look.

In this way and many others, Sephora is using technology to drive customer confidence in what was once the most analog of businesses. The company operates an innovation lab in San Francisco and is constantly testing new strategies. When I ask Laughton about what lies ahead for the company's digital strategy, she tells me there is no digital strategy: there is only a *customer* strategy.

"We start with the customer need," says Laughton. "We don't start with technology. We'll look at the need and ask, is there a role that technology or innovation can play to address this? For example, we don't have an AI [artificial intelligence] strategy. We have experiences that we're designing to meet consumer needs that may happen to use AI technology. That's the way we've got to think about it. We're really careful that we're not adding technology for the sake of introducing something new and shiny."

## MASTERING THE FUNDAMENTALS
## OF CUSTOMER CONFIDENCE

You don't have to be a Sephora-size business to make your customers feel confident in their interactions with you. Like everything else in sales, there is no one silver bullet. What follows are some fundamental techniques for driving customer confidence. Most don't cost a thing.

## Curate a manageable number of options.

Too much choice can be paralyzing and grind decision-making to a halt. If you've asked the right questions or have the right technology (like Sephora Color iQ), you should be able to narrow down your customers' product choices to a short list of recommendations. Curation is necessary to help drive customers toward buying decisions, and this is a prime way to demonstrate your knowledge and expertise.

## Don't do all the talking.

Build pauses into your conversations to give customers "airtime" to surface questions or concerns. Engage your customers with check-in questions throughout your conversations to make sure you're maintaining their attention. The more questions you ask, the more opportunities you have to provide great answers and build customers' confidence. On phone calls, where you have no visual cues, checking in with your customers is even more important. Ask questions such as

- "How does this sound so far?"
- "Does this meet your expectations?"
- "Do you have any questions I haven't addressed?"

Also, give your customers audible assurance that you're listening. This may not come naturally to everyone. Culturally, it's women who are expected to encourage speakers in conversation through actions such as head nods, "Mm-hmms," or reactive expressions, such as "That's interesting to hear." When working with women as customers, it's important for both male and female sales professionals to exhibit listening behaviors, whether in person or on the phone. Sometimes this can be as simple as repeating what your customer has said and demonstrating that you've understood her; for example, "I hear you loud and clear—we will not include delivery in our quote."

## Follow up quickly.

One of the top issues I hear from women is that sales professionals do not follow up, which is ironic when you consider that we've never had more ways to communicate with customers. Lack of follow-up is so pervasive that sometimes you can win a sale just by being the first—or only—person who follows up with a customer in a timely fashion. This means there are huge opportunities for people who are proactive, especially in industries with long sales cycles, where it may take ten or more interactions before a customer commits to buy. Follow-up builds trust, and trust builds sales.

## Understand how women define value.

You now know that for women, value doesn't necessarily mean the lowest price: it often means *what I bought is worth more than I paid for it*. Therefore, it's a good idea to underscore factors such as long-term value or resale value. Will your product last twenty years? Does it have a warranty? Will it add value to your customers' homes? Will it help them attract more talent to their business? Does it have versatility—can it be used to accomplish more than one thing? In both B2B settings and consumer sales, "making the business case" is especially important with women, who often represent a broad range of other people when making buying decisions. As such, they often find themselves not only factoring in other people's opinions but also explaining their decisions to others. Helping your customers recognize the value behind what you're selling—and not just the price—is one of the most important confidence builders there is.

## Provide key questions for customers to ask themselves.

One idea for setting yourself apart from competitors is to create a list of questions that customers should ask themselves before buying a product or service in your industry. These questions could be part of your sales collateral or marketing materials. Ideally, they will showcase your capabilities and frame your business as the right answer for someone's needs, because you will be able to answer yes to all of them. Here are some sample questions for an imaginary B2B company. Try to come up with five to ten for your own business.

1. Does the firm have global capabilities to help you enter new markets?
2. Does the firm offer quarterly updates to keep you apprised of progress?
3. Does the firm offer you educational resources and tools?

You see the pattern here—you are setting up your firm as the natural, smart choice.

## Remember that for women, the little things are the big things.

As we've seen throughout this book, details are credibility indicators for women buyers. One of the best strategies for instilling confidence is to focus on getting the details right. As previously mentioned, when you get the "small" things right, women are confident that you can be trusted with the big things—like their business. Here are some credibility indicators women may notice in your work:

- Proper spelling and grammar in your communications
- Correct name spelling
- Punctuality
- Following up when you say you will
- Cleanliness at retailers and offices
- A professional online presence

## Give your customer a "win."

Everyone's looking for a win, that little bit extra that makes someone feel that he or she has been given something above and beyond the purchase price. Giving your customer a "win" is especially important when you can't move on price. Here's a simple example: I was in the market for a new bicycle, and after I tested a new cruiser at a local shop, the store owner said, "If you buy this bike, I'll give you an ergonomic women's bike seat at no cost." He then handed me the bike seat for inspection. Logically, I knew the bike seat cost him little. In fact, it's likely he had already built the seat cost into the bike's price. However, in that moment, it felt like a win. This strategy can be motivating for your customer. "Wins" are also the kinds of things that women will mention to their friends and other networks. Plan them for talk value.

## Highlight all the value you personally bring to the table.

If you're in a service business, your customers probably don't realize all the things you do behind the scenes to add value to the product or service they're buying. How could they? Here's a great exercise for a slow day: write down all the things you do for customers that they may never see. Document this list, and when it's appropriate, bring up or show someone these activities to demonstrate the value you're providing. The "optics" on this can be phenomenal. If you don't do this, how else will your customer know what value you're personally bringing to the transaction?

## Ensure that you have a credible online presence.

Maintaining a professional online presence ranks right up there with breathing in terms of its importance to sales success. At the risk of understatement, if you don't have a professional online presence, you may be undermining your credibility, especially if you hope to attract young buyers. At a minimum, a professional online profile shows that you're a real person to prospects who haven't met you yet. More meaningfully, a professional profile communicates your credentials, the kinds of customers you serve, and a sense of your personality. "Buyers use social profiles to qualify the people they talk to," says Justin Shriber, vice president of marketing for LinkedIn Sales and Marketing Solutions, referring to a recent study of B2B buyers and sellers on the network.

"Before, it was primarily salespeople trying to learn about buyers. Now it's the opposite as well." If you haven't done so already, prioritize establishing a professional profile online, and use a high-quality photo that captures the type of image you want to convey to customers.

## Do one small thing to immediately demonstrate trustworthiness.

Credibility is built in both big and small ways, and most often it's the small ways that make the biggest impressions. Do this by accomplishing mini-commitments early in a client relationship. For example, if you tell a customer, "I will call you back in fifteen minutes," call back at exactly that time marker to demonstrate you can be trusted to do what you say you're going to do.

## Promote awards, accolades, and reviews.

There's a reason restaurants and hair salons cover their walls with media coverage of their businesses: it's instant credibility. Showcasing your own third-party awards, accolades, reviews, media coverage, and publicity can be an extremely credible way to build confidence in what you're selling.

Just a reminder here to be cautious of displaying sales awards if you're in financial services, health care, insurance, or any other industry where there is sensitivity to the idea of being "sold"—or even to the idea of being a "customer" (versus a patient, for example). Few people want to be reminded that they are a number in some-body's sales quota. If you're in one of these industries and you receive an award with the word "sales" in it from your company or a supplier, ask if the language can be rewritten to be more customer-centric, so you can display it without causing unease.

### Ask your customer if she has any concerns.

After you've engaged the interest of your customer, ask if she has any concerns about what you've discussed. By putting the question on the table, you have a chance to address any unspoken issues your customer may have, which gives you the opportunity to resolve them.

### Emphasize warranties, return or exchange policies, and the kind of service your customer can expect after the sale.

Women will often fast-forward to worst-case scenarios in high-stakes purchases. They weigh the risks and try to determine whether they can count on you to stand by the product should something go wrong.[2] This means it's important to proactively address the types of communication and service they can expect after the sale. Warranties, returns, and postsale service can be an important part of the confidence-building conversation; don't skimp on this information.

### Showcase the resources and team members behind you.

Showcasing the resources available to your customers can be a great confidence builder for them. If you have a team, communicate that they, too, are standing behind your customer, ready to provide support for any needs.

## Keep your customers in the know.

Information is social currency, and women tend to view themselves as lifelong learners. To maintain your status as an expert resource, build time in your day to read about customers, competitors, marketplace trends, and your industry. As much as you can, share trends and information with your customers, proactively send articles of interest, and consider writing/posting your thoughts on industry issues.

## Know your competition, and be prepared to articulate how you are different and better.

Be prepared to discuss how your product or service is meaningfully different from your closest competitors'. It's shocking how many people don't do this, or don't even know how they're different. I once mystery-shopped a home-building company and asked the sales consultant working in a model home, "What's the difference between your development and the subdivision across the street?" The answer: "They're pretty similar, I guess. It depends on what you want." Not exactly competitive differentiation. While we're here, the phrase "It depends on what you want" can make you sound disinterested, if you leave the words hanging in the air. But if you follow up with information about choices, you can instead inspire confidence.

## Talk about trade-offs to enhance your credibility.

Everything in life is a trade-off, and this goes for the products and services you're selling. Your customer already knows this. When you proactively bring up trade-offs between the options you offer, you show that you're not hiding any "gotchas," and this can increase your customers' confidence in your guidance.

## Let customers know how a product has improved over time.

If your product is something people only buy a handful of times in their lives, be sure to let them know how much it's changed for the better. If you grew up sleeping on your grandparents' lumpy pullout couch during summer vacations, for example, you might be hesitant to buy a sleeper sofa as a grown-up. Turns out, sleeper sofa beds are great now. Who knew? (The furniture industry, that's who.) There are so many products that have changed dramatically over the past decade. Your customer may have preconceived notions, rooted in past experiences, which could stand in the way of a sale. When appropriate, ask your customer about the last time she bought your product, and if it has significantly changed for the better since then, make sure she knows.

## Show customers how well you treat others.

Your customers are watching how you treat others. This doesn't just mean members of your own team; they're noticing how you treat everyone from restaurant servers to taxi drivers to administrative assistants. Demonstrate in all your actions that you are a courteous, kind person who deserves to be trusted with your customers' hard-earned money. This behavior gives your customer confidence that you will treat her well too.

## Manage mistakes in a way that inspires confidence for the future.

When you handle a mistake well, your customers can end up being more loyal to you than if a mistake had never occurred in the first place. I once met a grocery-store manager who fondly recalled one of his favorite mistakes, which had been made in the store's bakery department. A woman had ordered two cakes for a church event, and when she arrived to pick them up, there were mistakes on both. It had been a specialty order, so the customer was understandably upset. To make up for it, the manager apologized, waived the cost of both cakes, and then did something that earned her loyalty—and the business of her friends—for a very long time. He offered her two free cakes to bring to church every Sunday for the next month. The customer was so delighted that she spread word throughout the congregation. People from the church would stop the manager in the aisle to introduce themselves and thank him for the cakes. He gained new customers from that initial mistake; the way he handled it inspired confidence.

## Communicate while resolving mistakes.

Mistakes will always happen, and sometimes they can take several steps and time to sort out. Keeping people informed every step of the way, in terms of mistake management, is crucial. Withholding information compounds the problem and just makes people angry. We've all seen what happens at airports when an airline has a long delay and provides no details to the passengers; this is when mobs form. Regular communication helps defuse high-emotion situations and makes customers feel confident you are in control and working proactively on resolving the problem. Your customers want to feel like you are "on it."

## Build confidence in your pricing.

We live in a world in which customers can not only compare prices between providers, but in many cases they can learn (or make an educated guess on) the wholesale price that a company is paying for its products. This has changed the nature of negotiation for many businesses. A look at how one car manufacturer has adapted to the wide availability of car pricing online is instructive.

### BEST PRACTICE

### Lexus
*Building Customer Confidence at the Dealership*

For decades, haggling has been a stress point for car buyers, who have often lacked the confidence that dealerships will give them a fair price unless they fight tooth and nail for it. If you're a luxury automotive brand, how do you flip the script and earn customers' trust before they even walk through the dealership door? If you're Lexus, you revise the playbook.

Lexus has launched a breed of dealership, called "Lexus Plus," which offers up-front, negotiation-free pricing. At Lexus Plus dealerships—there are a dozen of them, as of this writing—the price listed on a vehicle is the price the customer pays. This means no haggling. No worrying that you're paying more than another customer for the same car. No *please-wait-here-while-I-get-my-manager*, because there's one point of contact for each customer.

I visited Rohrich Lexus in Pittsburgh, Pennsylvania, to see how this new dealership model works. "Our car-buying experience is now crafted around the guest, not the price," says Kevin Whalen, principal of Rohrich Automotive Group and a longtime owner of multiple dealerships. "Customers have the confidence that they're paying the same, competitive price without having to fight for it." Whalen has seen customer expectations shift dramatically over his years in the business. People spend nearly triple the amount of time searching for a car online than they do off line,[3] which means walking into a dealership has become a "moment of truth" for both buyer and seller. How has this changed the role of the sales professional?

"The era of 'Can I help you?' is over," says Whalen, referring to the standard greeting expected from sales professionals. "Technology raises the consumers' expectations. The sales professional has to be not only an expert on the vehicle, but also an expert on every aspect of the ownership experience from Lexus, not just the car."

With price off the table, Lexus Plus conversations shift from the topic of buying to the topic of *owning*. "I don't have to spend hours convincing a customer that Lexus is a great product," says Dave Clugston, a sales professional at Rohrich. "The customer already knows that. I need to let them *experience* it. My approach is to show them what it's going to be like to drive the car every day, and how easy it is to use features like voice technology. I'll introduce them to the service department and tell them that we'll be able to pick up their car and bring it in for appointments, to make it convenient for them. I tell my customers, 'All you need to do is drive it, and Lexus will take care of you.' Ultimately, I'm selling them on the experience of being a Lexus owner."

The combination of transparent pricing and a long-term ownership perspective has high appeal for women buyers. "Women express higher satisfaction with the Lexus Plus experience," confirms Peggy Turner, vice president of Lexus guest retention and satisfaction, citing data from participating dealerships across the United States. "They feel more in control with the up-front process than with the traditional buying experience. The guest works directly with one person throughout the entire purchase process. We also learned they're more likely to recommend purchasing from a Lexus Plus dealer."

Lexus Plus is an answer for building customer confidence when automotive pricing information is available all over the web, and customers—especially young ones—expect transparency from the companies with which they do business. Is it for everyone? No. At least not yet. For some people, haggling over the price of a car is a long-standing tradition, like eating turkey on Thanksgiving. But as with everything else in our transformational age, once people experience the ease and convenience of new options, and more importantly, *trust* them, broader adoption may follow. There are precedents, after all: used-car superstore CarMax built its empire on a haggle-free foundation. Saturn was a fixed-price operation before General Motors shut it down. Tesla and Costco are no-haggle sellers, as are a variety of dealerships of various makes throughout the United States.

As we have seen, instilling confidence in customers is a function of big things—like pricing strategy at Lexus Plus dealerships—and small things, like everyday personal interactions. How does one of the biggest dealmakers in commercial real estate instill confidence in clients? I asked her.

## BEST PRACTICE

## Q&A with Meredith O'Connor, International Director and Chairman of Headquarters Practice Group, JLL

Meredith O'Connor works on headline-making deals as a leader at real estate professional services firm JLL. She represented Toyota on the relocation of the company's North American headquarters from Torrance, California, to Plano, Texas, one of the biggest corporate moves in modern history. She also represented Toyota and Mazda on their high-profile selection of a $1.6 billion plant in Huntsville, Alabama, in 2018. A native Chicagoan, she represented the Barack Obama Foundation for the site selection of the Barack Obama Presidential Center in that city. No one works on deals at this level without earning the confidence of clients. I talked with O'Connor about how she does it.

*How would your clients describe you?*

I would hope they would say that I am a tireless advocate for their needs. I always put the client first.

*How do you differentiate yourself?*

I find that telling people you can save them money is an attention grabber, at least in terms of having them listen to what you have to say. But just as important is having a good story. The question you have to ask is, what is your best story about your work? How do you build it and make it your own? That is what life is about. One of my good stories is that we [JLL] know how to keep a secret. The Toyota move from Torrance to Plano was one of the best-kept economic development secrets in history. We kept the secret from start to finish.

*What is your work style?*

I'm a 24/7 kind of person. People in high-level positions expect responsiveness. The idea of "I'll get back to you within twenty-four hours" seems like an eternity now. It really should be a lot faster. I would never go to sleep at night without finishing today's emails, because it is just not acceptable anymore to wait any longer.

*How do you earn a client's trust?*

By protecting their interests, by doing everything you are told, and by always working your hardest to get them the best deal you can. That is what we did for Toyota, and that is why we have gotten the chance to work with them more than once.

*What is your client-engagement style?*

If someone asks me for three examples, I try to give them five. I think it is important that when somebody asks you to do something, you do just a little bit more, because that little bit more makes you better, and you are differentiating yourself from the average person. I have spent my life trying to do a little bit more, which is probably why I have five kids.

**What is your pet peeve?**

I hate when people have a message on the bottom of their email that says, "Please excuse the typos." I think it is a bad idea, because it just shows that they do not read what they send. To me, it's silly.

**What is one thing you never do?**

I never get involved in the negative. It takes energy to not get along with people. I always try to take the high road and get along with everyone. I think it is really important that people think you are a nice person. In this business that goes a long way.

## KEY TAKEAWAYS

- Giving customers a little bit more than they expect, as Meredith O'Connor does, can make a big impact on their impression of you.
- Customers' confidence increases when you successfully curate product choices, as Sephora does.
- Third-party credibility and an online professional presence are important for earning customers' confidence.
- Selling the experience of being your long-term customer,

as Lexus does, increases customers' confidence that they'll receive value beyond the product price.

## ACTIVATING YOUR INSIGHTS

- In what ways can you give your customers just 5 percent more than they're expecting (in terms of service), every time?
- Revisit your online professional profile. Is it up to date? Does it create a compelling impression of your capabilities? If you don't have a professional profile, make it a priority to create one.
- What analog activities in your own business could you bolster with technology, similar to the way Sephora uses technology to bolster customer confidence in its company and products?

## CHAPTER 7

# MOTIVATOR #4: APPRECIATED

*Make Your Customers Feel Appreciated for Their Business*

I'm visiting a bustling restaurant in the affluent Indianapolis suburb of Carmel, when a pair of regulars walks in and heads straight for my table. I can see they're not coming to talk to me, because they're looking straight at my companion, the restaurant's owner, John Liapes. It's an older couple, and they're all smiles as they say hello to him. When I'm introduced as a first-time visitor, they enthusiastically tell me this is their favorite place to eat. It's because of the way they're treated, they explain.

"John always stops by to talk with us, and every time Maria [the manager] sees us walk through the door, she brings out a newspaper to save our favorite table," the woman tells me. "Sometimes if Maria sees us coming from the parking lot, she has our meal on the table, waiting for us by the time we walk in." The woman looks me straight in the eye and says, "You can see why we love this place."

We are sitting in a McDonald's.

Liapes is a McDonald's owner/operator who came to the business from the world of fine dining, and it shows. As I sit in the Carmel location (one of his four McDonald's restaurants), it's hard to exaggerate how attractive it is: big picture windows, hardwood floors, textured walls, hanging light fixtures, sleek counters with charging outlets, artistic murals, and self-service kiosks. There are no ads or promotional window clings in sight. "I'm a purist," says Liapes, smiling. But it's not just the physical appearance of the restaurant that draws customers in; it's also how Liapes and his team, including his wife and business partner, Mary Liapes, treat their patrons and show them how much they value and appreciate their business.

## ANTICIPATING CUSTOMER NEEDS

"We train our teams to know what a guest needs before they do," Liapes says. "When we see moms walking in whose hands are full, for example, we need to assist them with getting seated and ensure that they have everything they need, so they don't have to get up and stand in line and leave their kids unattended. We're constantly doing things like bringing extra napkins to tables and refilling coffee, because people always need more napkins and more coffee. We want guests to walk away thinking, *They always pay attention to us, even when they're busy.*"

Needs anticipation is a key aspect of appreciation. Liapes calls it a *thoughtfulness connection.* He focuses his team's energy on these kinds of interactions because he believes they drive emotional engagement and long-term loyalty more than price promotions do. "It's more important for us to get the customer to come back than to get them to buy any individual thing," he says. "We don't want to be transactional with our guests; we want to be engaging. It's these thoughtful details that register with our guests, that are not expected and rarely executed in a quick service environment."

As the owner, Liapes isn't shy about showing customers how much he appreciates the opportunity to serve them. "I personally open the doors for customers, pick up trays, clean up the trash in the parking lot, and wipe down the glass doors," he says. "When guests see me doing that, they understand that someone has a vested interest in this restaurant succeeding, and doesn't take their business for granted."

## MASTERING THE FUNDAMENTALS OF APPRECIATION

As the restaurant experience with John and Mary Liapes shows us, appreciation has many dimensions beyond "thank you," such as anticipating your customers' needs. When you make customers feel appreciated, you increase your ability to close sales, develop repeat customers, and create word-of-mouth publicity. You already know that it's how you make people feel that motivates them to do business with you. The question is, are you making your customers feel appreciated? The following techniques are strategies to help you do so.

### Don't stop saying, "Thank you."

This is a friendly reminder to consistently say "please" and "thank you" as a matter of course. You'll notice that women have a habit of saying "thank you" first, even when they're the customer. Try to beat them to it. Note that the phrase, "Not a problem," is a poor substitute for "You're welcome" in a service-oriented business. Your customers may be thinking, *Yes, I know it's not a problem; it's your job.* Phrases such as, "My pleasure," "That's what I'm here for," or even simply "You're welcome," are more gracious.

## Give your full attention at the moment of payment.

The payment moment is often overlooked as an opportunity to make a lasting impression. If your customer is paying in person—as in a retail setting—train your teams to avoid taking phone calls, being distracted, or talking to each other about unrelated business during this period, to ensure each customer feels appreciated for spending her money with you. If you send invoices through email or snail mail, enclose a thank-you message.

## Find ways to celebrate a purchase.

You've closed the sale. How can you celebrate the moment with your customer? Is it worthy of a handwritten thank-you note, a gift, an event, a future discount on a purchase? Be creative. Small gestures make a lasting impression. In the era of junk mail and spam email, a handwritten thank-you note can stand out.

One of the best win-win thank-you practices I've heard about was from a woman who had recently remodeled her home. When the project was finished, her remodeling company did two things: first, it gave her a coffee table–worthy photo album of her project, featuring the company's logo on the cover, including before-and-after pictures. Second, the firm offered to pay for a party in her home, so she and her husband could invite friends and family to see the finished results. The party costs were capped at a relatively low dollar amount—enough to cover cake, snacks, and nonalcoholic drinks—and the offer came with one stipulation: that a representative of the firm (the one who handled her project) could attend the party and bring his business cards. The customer was thrilled with this arrangement and felt thanked and appreciated. The company, of course, was able to achieve a positive emotional outcome, while generating a new pipeline of future customers.

## There's no such thing as a tire kicker. Be courteous to browsers, and show you appreciate their interest.

If you believe that you're planting a seed with every person you meet—and you are—then no one is a tire kicker. Each person is yet another opportunity to make a great impression on someone, and you never know where it may lead. A customer could be browsing today but ready to buy tomorrow. And even if she never ends up buying a thing from you, a positive experience may lead her to refer you to others who will.

## If someone has spent a lot of money with you, follow up to show you care about the customer and not just the transaction.

If a customer has purchased a big-ticket item from you, follow up the next day (or the fastest speed appropriate) to check in, thank her, and provide her with some kind of communication that keeps the positive momentum going. The goal is to provide a measure of reassurance that you're not disappearing just because money has changed hands. Ultimately, this kind of fast follow-up reaffirms your commitment and helps prevent buyer's remorse or, worse, a return. Depending on your relationship, this second conversation may also give you the opportunity to ask for a referral or review, if your customer was happy with the experience.

## Provide elegant customer hand-offs.

Sometimes when a sale is made, there's a necessary hand-off to a different department or colleague in your organization. When these transitions are handled poorly, communication can break down and the customer feels as if customer service suddenly went from great to bad. Recommit to making sure these transitions go well. The experience is analogous to when you're talking with a customer service representative at a call center, and she tells you she needs to transfer your call to someone else. Your heart sinks unless the representative says, "I'll stay on the line with you and explain your situation to my colleague." An elegant hand-off is a thousand times better than a cold hand-off.

## Show that you remember previous conversations with your customer.

One of the strongest ways you can show appreciation for someone is to remember the things that she's told you. Saying something as simple as, "I remember, last time we spoke, you told me you were heading to a national conference in Orlando. How'd it go?" makes a positive impression. As human beings, we all have a deep need to be recognized and remembered. Remembering the names of children, spouses, and pets invariably generates goodwill. As soon as you learn these kinds of details, remember to record them in your contact database.

### Give them a reason to come back.

As McDonald's owner/operator John Liapes described, it's more important for customers to come back than to buy any individual thing. Tell your customers you look forward to working with them again and seeing them soon, and give them a reason to come back. They will feel good knowing you value their business.

### Consider creating a loyalty program, if you don't have one already.

Whether it's formal or informal, consider creating a customer loyalty program. Your goal would be to show appreciation to your customers by providing them with something of value above and beyond their purchases. The high-value items could be as simple as helpful content, such as thought-leadership articles and white papers, a discount for future purchases, invitations to special events, a reward program, exclusive first access to a new product, or something else altogether. To generate ideas, think of the loyalty programs you're already a member of yourself, and consider what makes them so compelling for you. When done effectively, you can build a *community* of customers that will enable you to solicit feedback, test ideas, and gather insights and data on purchasing patterns.

### Introduce your customers to people who could be helpful to them.

One higher-level way to show your appreciation to customers is to introduce them to people who could be helpful to their careers or interests. This could be done on a one-on-one basis, or you could take it even further by creating events, dinners, or other opportunities in which you bring like-minded customers to network with one another.

## Determine who your highest-volume customers are and, if you do nothing else, prioritize staying in close touch with them.

These loyal customers are yours to lose, so don't take any chances. Stay in touch with your most valuable customers through activities such as proactively visiting them, sending notes on topics that are of interest to them, commenting on their articles or promotional announcements on social networks, and sending holiday cards, birthday messages, or even anniversary messages that celebrate milestones. For example, a Realtor could send a note that says, "One year ago today, we closed on your new home. I hope you're enjoying it!" Thanks to technology and social media, it's easy to remember when significant events happened with your customers, and you may even have pictures to go along with the memory. Show that you're thinking about them, and they won't forget you. I've interviewed many sales professionals who've told me that their most effective marketing tool is a low-tech, handwritten note on a holiday card. Think it can't make a difference? One Allstate agent shows us how it can.

## BEST PRACTICE

## Allstate Agent Amy Maddox

Insurance is one of those rare products that people buy in the hopes that they'll never have to use it. This makes it challenging for insurance agents to engage and retain customers who may go years—or even a lifetime—without filing a claim. Since every customer must renew his or her policy (or not) annually, many people take that opportunity to shop around. Given this environment, how do the best agents retain customers while generating new ones? They consistently show appreciation to their clients and referrers. Just ask one of the "good hands people" at Allstate, who has a strategic approach to appreciation that can be adapted by anyone in client service.

Allstate is the largest publicly held personal lines property and casualty insurer in the United States, serving more than 16 million households.[1] For many of its customers, the company seems less like a corporate colossus and more like Bob or Shonda or Joe or Amy—the local agent who handles their business. In the United States, there are more than ten thousand Allstate agents, including Amy Maddox of Cedar Park, Texas, a suburb of Austin. Maddox is an award-winning "producer" (industry parlance for "agent") and alumnus of the national Allstate agent advisory board. For Maddox, demonstrating appreciation has been a key ingredient of her marketing strategy and sales success.

"Ninety percent of our business is word-of-mouth from current customers and mortgage companies," says Maddox, who owns and operates a seven-person firm, the Maddox Insurance Company, which is an exclusive Allstate agency. Staying top of mind and driving referrals requires constant proactivity, because "the days of meeting your insurance agent face-to-face are gone," she explains. "Although we welcome people to come into the office, they often just don't have time anymore, so we have to find other ways to show we value them."

Maddox and her team put a lot of energy into showing appreciation through phone calls and emails, their two primary sources of customer communication. "We are not transactional," says Maddox. "When people call in, we ask how they are and we mean it. People want to know that you are listening to them and that you hear what they're saying. We tell our customers over and over again that we're here for you, we're local, and if you need us, you could walk into our office. They might never walk in the door, but they like knowing that they could."

Maddox and her colleagues send handwritten, personal notes for their customers' major life events, like the birth of a baby or death of a spouse. They send birthday cards. They send Thanksgiving cards with messages of thanks for being a customer. When someone refers a new client, they send a gift card and a handwritten note. All new customers receive thank-you emails five days after they've purchased a policy. The email includes a photo of the entire Maddox team, with a message that every staff member is at the customer's disposal. The goal is to make each customer feel personally welcomed and valued by the firm.

A business built on referrals doesn't happen overnight. Maddox has been remarkably consistent in demonstrating appreciation to a key community of influencers: one hundred local mortgage brokers with whom she's built strong relationships over the course of her career. These people are the most important referral pipeline for her business.

"Every month for almost twenty years—with the possible exception of when I was pregnant—I've taken marketing gifts to these mortgage people," she says. "I always do something very simple. For example, this month it's Easter, so we're sending a chocolate Easter egg with a note that says, 'Thank you for the eggcellent referrals.'"

Every month.

With a different thank-you message.

For twenty years.

*Now, that's a consistent demonstration of appreciation.*

"I still personally deliver the gifts myself, because talking to people is how I build relationships," says Maddox. If by now you're thinking, *That's a lot of thanking,* yes, it is. But appreciation that's unexpressed may not be felt, which means demonstrating it requires proactivity. And proactivity takes time.

Maddox and her fellow agents are supported at Allstate headquarters with a corporate team that works to innovate processes so that agents can spend more time on relationship-building activities. "One of our goals is to build tools and leverage technology that help take low-value-added activities out of our agents' hands, so they can spend more time on the high-touch, high-value activities," says Gannon Jones, senior vice president of consumer marketing at Allstate. "At the end of the day, even with unprecedented technology and data, we're still developing products and services for human beings who have feelings and emotions. The best companies recognize that it's still a balance of art and science."

---

At the opposite end of the spectrum for a low-interest category like insurance is the high-interest world of luxury fashion. We all know how hard it is to find a thank-you gift for someone who "has everything." Now expand that thought and imagine being in the luxury business, where you're faced with the challenge of showing appreciation to a jet-setting, global customer base that can afford to take its business anywhere. How do you show appreciation to this kind of clientele? If you're one of the 150 brands in Milan, Italy's MonteNapoleone District, you join forces with your competitors, to take your efforts to places that would be out of reach on your own.

## BEST PRACTICE

## Luxury Brands Join Forces to "Scale" Appreciation

Milan's legendary shopping avenue, Via Montenapoleone, is filled with some of the most exclusive brands in the world. Prada, Gucci, Giorgio Armani, Salvatore Ferragamo, Loro Piana, and dozens of others line this stately street and the surrounding neighborhood. More than 25,000 people per day visit this shopping district, and 80 percent come from outside of Europe. The area has the highest average ticket spend among the main shopping streets in the world.[2] Brands here compete with other fashion capitals around the globe to court the business of a luxury clientele. To do this more effectively, the MonteNapoleone District has created a program called "One Luxury Destination," in collaboration with the consulting firm Accenture.

"These brands are usually competitors, but in this case they're allies," says Umberto Andreozzi, fashion and luxury digital lead at Accenture.[3] Working together as the MonteNapoleone District association, these brands use their collective resources to provide exclusive customer experiences in a distinctly Italian style.

Interested in spinning around Lake Como in a Ferrari? Care to go truffle hunting in Alba, Italy? Perhaps you'd enjoy relaxing in a VIP lounge in a stately villa, champagne in hand, with a personal shopper bringing you every red dress in your size from every store in the area, if that's what your heart desires. These are the kinds of experiences the association delivers.

"The individuals who are visiting MonteNapoleone are global travelers," says Guglielmo Miani, president of the MonteNapoleone District and CEO and president of Larusmiani, the oldest luxury clothing and tailoring brand on Via Montenapoleone. "They are always looking for the coolest and best experiences in the world. They don't want to be bored." While the experiences are always changing, the One Luxury Destination program has three fundamentals:

*First-of-Its-Kind VIP Lounge.* The MonteNapoleone VIP lounge is the first in the world to service a "fashion district," and it represents the physical heart of the One Luxury Destination collaboration. Housed in a beautiful, historic palace right on Via Montenapoleone, this lounge has the feel of a luxurious, private club. (I visited in the name of research.) Admittance is by invitation only and mostly reserved for the brands' best customers. Once inside, customers find a twenty-four-hour concierge service, personal shoppers, private dressing rooms, lounge areas and refreshments, services such as free baggage transfer to the airport (to help with all those new shopping purchases), airport check-in for extra baggage (more help with all those new purchases), a butler at the airport, as well as processing of VAT tax refunds, so customers don't have to stand in line at the airport.

*A Concierge Service.* A dedicated concierge service is offered both in person (at the MonteNapoleone VIP Lounge) and online. The concierge will make personal appointments with customers' favorite brands, organize chauffeur services, handle customer requests, such as making dinner reservations at high-end restaurants, organizing private dining experiences, making hotel reservations, scheduling tours, and securing tickets for activities such as concerts, fashion shows, and the opera. For example, if a customer would like to tour the Ferrari factory, they can make it happen. If someone is more excited by motorsports events at nearby Monza, this too can be arranged. Let's say a customer is more of a palaces and museums kind of person; they can provide special access exclusively for MonteNapoleone VIP Lounge guests.

*"Digitized Streets" Website and App.* One Luxury Destination features a dedicated website and app designed to help customers begin their immersion into the glamorous heart of Milan before they even leave home, and keep it going long after they say ciao.

---

The bottom line? As businesses as diverse as McDonald's, Allstate, and the MonteNapoleone District show us, customer appreciation never goes out of style, no matter what business you're in or what type of clientele you serve.

## KEY TAKEAWAYS

- Making customers feel appreciated takes time and effort, but it's well worth it in terms of increased customer loyalty and referrals.
- Appreciation has many dimensions behind thank you: It also includes elements such as anticipating customer needs and celebrating purchases.
- Consistent follow-up is one of the most important ways to demonstrate appreciation for someone's business. It shows the customer that her business wasn't considered a mere "transaction."

## ACTIVATING YOUR INSIGHTS

- What are some creative ways you can show appreciation to your customers? You don't have to break the bank. In my neighborhood, two nail salons are on the same street. One offers a free, two-minute shoulder massage with each manicure, and one doesn't. Guess which one gets my business?
- If you created a loyalty program for your business, what could it look like?

- Identify the obstacles that prevent you from keeping in regular touch with customers and influencers. What can you do to make this process more manageable?

## CHAPTER 8

# TOP TRENDS DRIVING WOMEN'S BUYING PATTERNS

*A Road Map to Exceeding Customer Expectations*

N ow that we've firmly established The Four Motivators Framework and how it helps drive engagement with women customers, let's turn our attention in another direction: the macro trends driving women's lifestyles and purchasing patterns. While the four motivators are timeless principles that will remain effective for years to come, it's important to stay in tune with what's currently happening in women's lives that impact their wants and needs. These trends provide timely context for the four motivators that will help ensure your ideas and strategies are relevant to women's lives.

There are six major trends impacting women's buying patterns. Separately, these trends are like dots on a map, but when you piece them together, they create a road map of where your customers are going and how you can develop strategies to stay ahead of their needs. When combined with the four motivators, they give you a complete picture of how to better understand and serve this market.

## TREND #1: DOUBLE DUTY, HALF THE TIME

The mother of all trends is what I call "Double Duty, Half the Time." It describes the blurred lines between work life and home life and the resulting time compression that comes from it—the feeling that we have less time. Each one of us has the same twenty-four hours in a day that our cave-dwelling ancestors had, but thanks to our multitasking lives and the technology that tethers us, it often feels as though we have less than that—and this drives how, when, and with whom women choose to do business.

First, let's place our busy lives in some historical context. Before the industrial revolution, work life and home life were largely one and the same. Men, women, and children worked together in their homes on the shared goal of family survival. They used their land for growing food and raising animals. They used their houses to prepare meals and provide shelter from the elements. And they sold everything extra to generate income. It wasn't until the advent of factories that home and work started to be viewed as separate concepts.[1] Ironically, the age of technology has brought us back to this fusing of work and home life. Instead of pounding grain at our kitchen tables, we're now answering emails, writing PowerPoint decks, or running businesses from them instead.

Modern women often experience time compression acutely, because so many of them are balancing work with caregiving roles. When you think about serving a market of working women, it can be helpful to think that many are working two jobs: the one they get paid for, if they work outside of the home, and the one they don't get paid for, inside the home or in caregiving roles with elderly parents or in-laws. The result is that women often have less time to engage in shopping and buying. And when time for shopping goes down, expectations for ease and convenience go up: it's an inverse relationship.

There is less patience (and often no patience whatsoever) for interacting with companies or salespeople who are not elegantly easy to work with. The less time your customer has, the more she values it—and the more she values the people who respect it and save it.

## It's All About Execution

For a vivid example of the Double Duty, Half the Time life-style, let's turn to Judi, a busy executive from New York. It's a Tuesday in Manhattan, and I'm sitting across the table from Judi in a crowded coffee shop. She's the kind of person who exudes competence, and the minute she starts talking, I feel compelled to straighten my posture, smooth my clothes, and pay attention. Judi doesn't waste words or time, and listening to how she runs her life as a single parent is like a master class on efficiency. I ask her to tell me how she makes her life work.

"It's all about execution," says Judi, who runs her own consulting business and the lives of her two elementary school-age children. "I have a lot to pull off in a day, and I don't have time to strike out."

I put down my pen when she says, "I don't have time to strike out." Let this be a lesson to all of us: when women are in the marketplace, they *want* to execute. They want to be productive. They want to get the job done. They don't want to leave empty-handed. Judi lists her responsibilities on a typical day:

- job/client work
- food procurement

- cleaning
- dog care and dog walking
- repairs of any and every kind
- getting kids ready for school
- getting kids to school
- medical care for herself and the kids
- veterinary care

"I'm in charge of every department," Judi says. She takes a breath and rattles off all the apps she used on a recent morning, while sitting in the back of a cab on her way to JFK airport for a business trip. As she speaks, I feel the kind of awe typically reserved for Cirque du Soleil performances. That morning, Judi used apps to

- schedule her dry-cleaning pickup,
- organize multiple dog walks with a hired dog walker,
- order dinner for her children,
- hire someone to assemble a desk she ordered from IKEA,
- buy flood insurance, because a hurricane was on its way to New York, and
- order new clothes for her kids.

Did I mention that she accomplished all this before she boarded a morning flight? And did you see the part where she bought flood insurance?

Judi takes my astonishment in stride. "Using these apps is not about a shortcut: it's about a *way*. I'm relying on tech heavily. I need to execute on the tasks in the most efficient way possible, to clear a path so that I can do the things that only I can do."

Judi's experiences paint a picture of why it's now "table stakes" to be easy and convenient to work with, no matter what business you're in. The other side of this is, of course, the opportunity to cater to this new appetite for helpful services. Consider the list of apps Judi used on a single morning. They were mostly service-based. When I interview women, they often tell me they have plenty of stuff, and what they're looking for is more help.

Halfway across the country from Judi, a woman named Jen gives me a simple but compelling example of what helpful and convenient looks like from her perspective. She tells me about one of the first times she left her house to go shopping shortly after having a baby.

"I remember my first time pulling in to the Nordstrom parking lot with a colicky baby and almost tearing up when I saw they had spaces designated for 'new parent' parking. I thought, *Oh my God. Someone gets me. Someone cares about my experience here.*" Nordstrom literally put up signs telling their customers they were trying to make it easy for them to do business with the company.

In the Double Duty, Half the Time world, being easy, efficient, and convenient will capture the attention of busy women who are looking for your help in achieving their goals, and increase the chances that your customers will feel connected, inspired, confident, and appreciated.

## KEY TAKEAWAYS

- Being easy and convenient to work with is now "table stakes" for serving a market of modern women. If your business isn't helpful, convenient, and easy to work with, you'll eventually be disrupted by a competitor that is.[2]
- Busy women are looking for services and not just products.

## ACTIVATING YOUR INSIGHTS

- Many of the apps that Judi uses provide a helpful service, not a product. Could you offer a complementary service for the products you sell? For example, IKEA bought TaskRabbit, an app-based business that helps people with errands and activities such as assembling IKEA furniture. It was a natural match. Ulta Beauty stores offer a variety of hair and beauty treatments. How else can you make your customers' lives easier with a service that complements your products? Can you leverage new technologies to offer conveniences such as deliveries and automatic replenishment?
- Time is only one aspect of convenience. Write a list of other aspects of convenience that you can provide through your business.

## TREND #2: THE MINI-ME EFFECT

I had just chosen my nail color when it happened. "Please take a seat," said the manicurist, as she motioned to the small chair. It was rush hour at the salon, around five thirty on a Thursday. As is my custom, I gave a head nod and brief eye contact to the client seated next to me. I hoped my face didn't betray my surprise when I registered the fact that the customer sitting next to me was an eleven-year-old girl.[3]

Getting her nails done professionally.

On a weeknight.

I shouldn't have been surprised. Have you noticed? Kids are now engaged in adult activities and adult brands more than ever—the kind that you once had to grow up to get.

Welcome to the Mini-Me Effect, the new world order in which adults and kids actively want and use the same products, brands, and services. It's now increasingly hard to answer the questions, "What's a product or service for kids?" and "What's a product or service for grown-ups?"

The line between them is slowly being erased.

Kids love the brands their parents love (Exhibit A: Converse), grandparents love the brands their kids love (Exhibit B: Starbucks), and everyone from age eight to eighty wants the same technology (Exhibit C: iPads).[4] Many kids no longer have to wait until they're grown up to get the products and services their parents enjoy. No doubt you've witnessed this. Maybe you've found yourself strolling past a five-year-old in the business-class section of a flight to Orlando, flying on his parents' miles. Perhaps you've walked

into a hair salon near prom time and seen young girls getting professional blowouts and makeup applications. Maybe your teenage
nephew asked you to pick up a latte for him on your way to his
house. When I'm out conducting retail research, I routinely see
mothers and daughters eyeing the same designer purses.

Previous generations were mortified by their parents' taste in
just about anything. What's different now? Everything. The root
of it is this: people are getting married later in life, which means
they are often having children later in life, after they've been
working for years and earning money. Then if they have children,
they have fewer of them than previous generations. Having fewer
kids later in life has a domino effect on family lifestyles. For one
thing, there are now more dual-income parents who can distribute
their resources across fewer children. And parents with means are
often willing and able to spend the kind of adult-sized money on
their kids that previous generations either couldn't or wouldn't.

Let's imagine the scenario of a woman—we'll call her Tracy—
who gets pregnant with her first child at thirty-four, an age that
is no longer unusual for young motherhood. By the time she's
thirty-four, Tracy's had at least twelve years of establishing an
income and lifestyle before a baby enters the picture, and so
has her husband. By that time, she's been going to Starbucks for
longer than she can remember; manicures have become a routine
event, no longer reserved for special occasions; she earns air miles
for frequent flying and credit card spending; and she has long ago
traded up to better brands than she and her husband could afford
when they were in their twenties.

Once they have a baby, the child naturally becomes a part of her parents' world. As a result, Tracy's daughter has been going to Starbucks since she was in a stroller and will not wait for her wedding day to get her first manicure. She's already had plenty of them, many of which have served as a treat for accompanying her mom to the nail salon. And since Tracy is a working mom, she is always looking for ways to spend free time in the company of her daughter.

Kids are involved in family decision-making more than ever. This is particularly true in single-parent households. And when it comes to product research, some kids consider themselves to be the Google "researchers in chief" for their households, in addition to the resident tech experts.

If you're in a consumer business, it's worth looking at the opportunity that could come from embracing younger consumers, assuming your product is appropriate for buyers under eighteen. Successful examples of brand extensions are everywhere you look: from Athleta Girl to CLIF Kid Zbars to Baby Dior, to resorts that feature kids "camps" and clubs. There are some powerful forces working in your favor when you do embrace young buyers: you're appealing to parents with means who are willing to spend adult-size money on their kids, and kids who want to engage in the same brands and activities that their parents do. And lest you think this trend is occurring only in the worlds of salons, fashion, and technology, it's not. Just look at your local golf course.

## The Mini-Me Effect in Golf: A Sport That's Also a Service Business

From the outside, golf is a glamorous and graceful sport, played in the world's most beautiful locations. From the inside, it's a service business that must cultivate the next generation of players to thrive and grow. The people on the front lines of delivering player experiences are the 29,000 PGA of America (PGA) Professionals working at courses and clubs throughout the United States. From providing lessons to running golf shops, courses, and clubs, they're in the business of delivering great player experiences that inspire amateurs like us to take lessons, join clubs, and renew memberships. So how are they reaching out to the next generation of golfers? They're tapping into the power of the parent-child connection.

"Women are key to the next generation of golfers," says Sandy Cross, senior director of diversity and inclusion for the PGA of America. This is because mothers typically play a strong role in determining their children's recreational activities. Cross's goal is to bring more players from all types of backgrounds into the sport. Making this a reality are people like PGA Professional Ernie Ruiz, director of golf at Lago Mar Country Club in Plantation, Florida.

Ruiz tells me that earlier in his career, he created a junior program designed to get kids out on the golf course. Something unexpected happened along the way: he got the parents out too. "I drove out to watch our kids in a clinic and saw all these parents sitting around with nothing to do," says Ruiz, who was working at a different club in Florida at the time. "So we created a tag-along clinic for the parents. A lot of them hadn't played golf before. They were out there supporting their kids, but they weren't necessarily golfers. The clinic gave them a first step into the game."[5] Voilà: the creation of parallel programming to cater to parents and kids at the same time.

There are so many possibilities for parallel programming in service businesses. Think about hair salons providing parallel appointments for parents and kids. Or gyms offering tumbling classes for kids, while Mom or Dad attends a yoga class at the same time—instead of sitting in their cars, killing time before pickup. Are there opportunities for your business to leverage the Mini-Me Effect?

## KEY TAKEAWAYS

- Unlike previous generations, parents and kids now often want the same brands, products, and services. The potential for business growth through "age elasticity" exists in many products and services, thanks to the Mini-Me Effect.
- Kids are more active and engaged in family decision-making than in previous generations. They are brand aware at a young age, and as digital natives, some kids regard themselves as product "researchers in chief" for their households.

## ACTIVATING YOUR INSIGHTS

- Consider how this trend could be an opportunity for your business to grow. Does it make sense for your brand to move up or down the age spectrum? Is there an opportunity to provide "parallel programming" for both kids and parents?

- Pets are a part of the family too, and a fast-growing sector of the consumer economy. Determine whether your business has an opportunity here too.

## TREND #3: VISUAL STORYTELLING

Life has become one big photo opportunity waiting to happen. Thanks to social media, many people walk around with a mental "shot list" in their heads, constantly framing scenes that would make great photos or videos to post online. (They're thinking of captions too.) Using the cameras in our phones, we are all shooting the documentary of our own lives—and then, we're often posting it. With women dominating the biggest social networks, how can your business be a part of the visual storytelling trend and inspire people to document their purchases and experiences with your company?

It made international news when a five-star resort in the Maldives began offering "Instagram butlers" to help guests capture the perfect shot for their social media networks.[6] In retrospect, the idea of Instagram butlers seems like an inevitability. When someone buys a product or has an experience that she views as particularly exciting or important, she often tells the story through pictures and videos, so much that it's almost as if we could ask a new type of existential question: If you bought something really exciting but didn't post a picture of it, *did you really buy it?*

I have a friend who's a Realtor in Texas, and every time he closes on a house, he posts a picture with his clients standing next to him. The clients always hold a sign that says some version of "My Realtor is a rock star!" I once visited a hotel in Los Angeles that had a red carpet and a large banner at the entrance. I assumed there was a special occasion happening there that night and asked the valet what it was. The answer was that there was no special occasion. The banner and red carpet were there to make every guest feel like a celebrity—and, of course, provide an irresistible backdrop for pictures to post on social media.

Our propensity to tell visual stories has led to the creation of new "mini milestones" that women document to share even the smallest of life's moments. These, too, provide an opportunity for you to get creative. For example, we're all accustomed to seeing photos about traditional life milestones, such as the purchase of a new house, the first day of school, a new baby, a new marriage, a new car. But there is a whole swath of "mini" milestones that are now catalysts for visual storytelling, such as baby gender reveals, weekly and monthly "birthday" pictures of new babies, filmed and photographed marriage proposals, completion of a home décor or craft project, the finish line of a 5K run, and so many more. A quick scroll through your social network feeds would likely produce dozens of other examples. How can your business or brand be a part of your customers' mini milestones, or help them create new ones?

Domino's Pizza offers a great example: the company has an online *baby registry* (a baby registry!) that promotes the idea of sending pizzas to new and expecting parents, to help them celebrate mini milestones with funny and engaging messages, such as "Sleeping Through the Night—Trust us. It's a reason to celebrate"; "The Gender Reveal—Either is worth a celebration"; and

"Hormonal and Hangry—The struggle is real."[7] In your own business, how can you be a part of women's visual storytelling and get in the picture for big milestones, mini milestones, and their purchases of your product?

## KEY TAKEAWAYS

- We have become a world of visual storytellers, shooting the documentaries of our own lives. Our tool is the smartphone; our medium is the social network.[8]
- No life milestone is too small to film, photograph, or post. This is often true for purchases too, which presents an opportunity for every brand and business.

## ACTIVATING YOUR INSIGHTS

- Brainstorm creative ways to inspire customers to include you, your products, or your services in their social media posts.
- How can you be a part of the new wave of mini milestones in our culture?

## TREND #4: HEALTH AND WELLNESS AS A LIFESTYLE

"Is it good for me or bad for me?"

That's the kind of question that was once reserved for buying food and pharmaceuticals. Not anymore. Wellness has gone mainstream. It's emerged as a key component for consumer decision-making across industry categories,[9] whether we're talking about allergy-friendly paints, vegan shampoos, or SPF-infused swim shirts. The emphasis on wellness has particular relevance to women, who make 80 percent of health-care decisions for their families and are the consumer force driving the health and wellness revolution.[10]

Broadly speaking, wellness is a concept that encompasses everything from health and fitness to spirituality, eco-friendliness, and mind and body enrichment. Given the enormity of this macro trend, it's worth asking: Are there untapped attributes of health and wellness in your own business? Bringing them to life could mean added sales, market share, and reasons to buy. It certainly has for Westin Hotels, and there are many insights from the brand's innovation in this category that can serve as inspiration for yours.

## Wellness at Westin

The launch of the Westin Heavenly Bed in 1999 made an entire generation rethink their lodging choices. Westin Hotels & Resorts, one of Marriott International's marquee brands, has anchored its brand in wellness since that iconic marketing moment. The bed was a revolutionary move obvious only in retrospect: differentiate a hotel chain by promising a great night's sleep. The legacy of the Heavenly Bed—and the bed itself—endures as a testament to the customer-experience transformation of the modern hotel industry.

*Legacy #1:* Heavenly Beds were launched with white duvet covers, a bold move in an industry that had long relied on dark, patterned blankets to hide stains. White linens signaled to guests that they could have supreme confidence in the beds' cleanliness. The entire industry followed suit: white linens are now standard in upscale hotels.

*Legacy #2:* Westin was happy to sell you the bed if you liked it, down to the pillows and sheets. This was an extraordinary concept at the time. To this day, you can buy the Heavenly Bed and other signature items from Westin hotels, including the soothing scent of its lobbies.

The idea of sleeping well was the start of a broader commitment by Westin to wellness in all forms. The brand's guest experience is now founded on six pillars of well-being that have high appeal to modern consumers—especially women. The Six Pillars are:

- Sleep Well
- Eat Well
- Move Well
- Feel Well
- Work Well
- Play Well

"Our goal is to help guests leave the hotel feeling better than when they arrived," says Brian Povinelli, senior vice president and global brand leader for Westin.

### Helping Travelers Stay on Their Fitness Routines

Let's say you've forgotten your workout gear while you're traveling or couldn't squeeze it into a bag without checking it. Westin features a program in which you can borrow New Balance clothes, shoes, and new socks—in sizes for both women and men—for a nominal fee, and you get to keep the socks. No more stuffing those bulky sneakers into a small suitcase.

"We started that program right around the time the airlines were starting to charge for checked baggage," says Povinelli. "We noticed that a lot of people were leaving their workout gear behind. So we partnered with New Balance and came up with a solution." As a bonus, guests don't have to pack dirty, sweaty clothes to bring home.

Now let's say you've put on those New Balance loaner sneakers and want to head out for a run but don't know where to go. After all, you live out of town. Westin created the position of "run concierge" in many of its locations (two hundred concierges and growing) to lead group runs for guests. If you're the type of person who prefers to run solo, you can simply follow one of the running routes that Westin and New Balance have mapped out for each one of the hotel's locations.

Inside the hotels, there's been an emphasis on the design and expansion of gyms. "Historically, hotel fitness centers were often repurposed guest rooms—dark rooms with carpets and low ceilings," says Povinelli. "We've been a leader in shifting the paradigm: our Westin Workout Studios have more of the feel of a third-party gym. All of them feature TRX equipment, and many of our hotels feature Peloton bikes that guests can reserve in advance."

Fitness is just one aspect of the wellness platform. Westin also offers a "super foods" menu created in partnership with SuperFoodsRx, workspaces and meeting rooms designed to enhance productivity, and even a "Sleep Well Lavender Balm" that guests can rub onto their temples or wrists before bedtime to help ease them into a sound slumber. The list is long.

"We're offering five to fifteen programs under each pillar," says Povinelli. Because your idea of wellness may differ from mine, Westin caters to a wide variety of needs.

## KEY TAKEAWAYS

- Health and wellness are powerful motivators for women's decision-making, across industries.
- There are a vast number of ways to bring health and wellness to life, because "wellness" can be defined so broadly.

## ACTIVATING YOUR INSIGHTS

- Identify the health and wellness trends influencing your customers right now. Are there any latent health and wellness qualities you can tap into within your own business?
- In what ways can you demonstrate that your product or service is "good for you"? Write down as many as possible.

## TREND #5: SIXTY IS THE NEW FORTY

My friend Gina loves to joke that she'll receive her AARP card while her kids are still in elementary school. For those of you unfamiliar with AARP, it's the organization formerly known as the American Association of Retired Persons; its membership cards are infamous for showing up in US mailboxes on or around someone's fiftieth birthday. Gina gave birth in her late thirties and early forties. She's fifty now and laughs at the thought of getting retirement messages at a life stage when she's still hosting action hero–themed birthday parties and saving for her kids' college tuitions.[11]

Gina is a perfect example of how relying on age to define someone's lifestyle and spending patterns can be misleading, especially when it comes to women. Life stage is a much greater predictor of a woman's wants and needs than the date on her birth certificate. That fifty-something woman down the street could be an empty nester with grown-up kids, or the mother of an elementary-school child, or she could have no children at all. With increased singlehood, "gray divorce," later marriages, delayed childbirth, delayed household formation, and the phenomenon of multiple acts in our careers and personal lives, the old rules about what characterizes a sixty-year-old, for example, no longer apply.

But stereotypes die hard, so let's try to debunk some right here: people ages fifty and older, which includes members of Generation X, hold a whopping 83 percent of US household wealth.[12] They dominate all consumer spending in the United States,[13] in categories including nondurable goods, durable goods, utilities, motor vehicles and parts, financial services, health care, and household goods.[14] Women drive consumer spending in this age group as they do in all other groups, though you'd never know it by the images we see in campaigns.

Culturally, we know that men with gray at the temples are often viewed as "distinguished," while many older women are not viewed at all. Literally. Based on my research, and the research of many others, women fifty-five and older often describe themselves as feeling largely invisible in the marketplace. Mature women report that they often receive little eye contact and even less attention as customers. Not taking these women seriously is a big mistake.

When it comes to mature women in the consumer market-place, the empty-nesting phase is a time when many feel they can finally put their own needs first. I call women in this life stage the "make your own darn dinner" generation. It can be an exciting time of life. In my interviews, I routinely hear women say things like, "I've taken my son Tommy's old bedroom and turned it into my office." "I'm planning the kind of vacations I've always wanted to have." "I'm getting rid of my junky living room furniture and getting something nice." I've met many women in this age group who travel frequently with girlfriends because their husbands aren't interested. They don't let that stop them.

And, yet, few businesses approach this market as if maturity is an exciting period in people's lives. Pay attention long enough, and you get the impression that marketing and selling to older audiences consists almost entirely of somber—and often patronizing—pitches for health care, adult diapers, supplements, and financial services.[15] There's little acknowledgment that an enormous part of the over-fifty-five market is youthful, active, and engaged, and becoming entrepreneurs at virtually the same rate as millennials.[16] There's a gap for products and services delivered with style, coolness, and enthusiasm for the future.

And who has stepped in to fill that gap? None other than Jimmy Buffett.

Yes, you read that right: Jimmy Buffett, the singer and business tycoon famous for building an empire on the fantasy of escaping to the tropics with a margarita in one hand and a cheeseburger in the other. His company opened the first Margaritaville-themed retirement community for people aged "55 and better" in 2018.

## Reimaging This Stage of Life as Margaritaville

The official name of the retirement community created by Buffett's company is Latitude: Margaritaville, and it's a place where people can "grow older but not up," as one of Buffett's song lyrics goes. The initiative is a partnership between Margarita Holdings, LLC (the restaurant, hotel, and leisure company in which Buffett is the majority stakeholder) and Minto Communities USA, a homebuilder with more than sixty years in the business. Call it cheeseburgers—and aging—in paradise. As of this writing, there are two locations under development: Daytona Beach, Florida, and Hilton Head, South Carolina. A third location is being planned for Watersound, Florida, in the state's panhandle region.

The communities promise a tropical lifestyle filled with beach cabanas, thatched-roof bars, and live music every day. There's even an interactive dog park and pet-grooming spa called Barkaritaville. With the announcement of Latitude: Margaritaville, Jimmy Buffett and company suddenly made it cool to be in a retirement community, a feat that (arguably) no one else has accomplished. That's because they're not just selling a place to live: they're selling a state of mind.

"We're turning the active-adult segment on its ear," says William Bullock, senior vice president of Minto Communities USA, and the lead executive overseeing the development. "The idea that older people want the early-bird special, go to bed at 6:00 p.m., and are in heaven's waiting room—none of that is true. It's the opposite of what we're experiencing with this buyer group. These people want to socialize, have fun, and continue to enrich themselves through education. They're energetic, they're social, they're focused on wellness and fitness, and they like to travel."

As this book went to press, more than 120,000 people had registered to get updates on the Latitude: Margaritaville project. And not all of these people are "Parrotheads"—the term for serious Jimmy Buffett fans. In fact, the company's internal research shows that 75 percent of people in the database have never been on the corporate Margaritaville website, a popular destination for Buffett fans. What this means is that Latitude: Margaritaville has tapped into a much broader market. The community's leasing office in Daytona Beach is so popular it's become a kind of tourist attraction.

### It's Five O'Clock Somewhere

When I heard about Latitude: Margaritaville, I had to see it with my own eyes. So off I went to Daytona Beach, just a few weeks after the community's first residents moved in. The community is in the heart of golf country here, and as Bullock drove me down LPGA Boulevard the first thing I saw was a lifeguard tower—the symbol of Daytona Beach—marking the entrance to the community. We pulled into a charming neighborhood of pastel-colored homes in beach-cottage styles. Construction crews were everywhere. As we got out of the car, I heard music from the Beach Boys being piped throughout the community on Sirius XM's Radio Margaritaville stream, setting the mood for prospective buyers. Model home tours start under a thatched-roof structure at the top of a street. The sensory engagement and brand infusion in this community is evident in every detail. Here are a few examples of how the brand is brought to life in the experience:

## Street Names
- Flip Flop Court
- St. Somewhere Drive
- Tiki Terrace
- Island Breeze Avenue

## Home Model Names
- Aruba
- Bimini
- St. Bart
- Nevis

## Amenities
- Fins Up! Fitness Center
- Barkaritaville
- Last Mango theater
- Latitude Town Square
- Paradise Pool
- 5 O'Clock Somewhere Bar

With sixty-nine hundred homes (in the Daytona Beach project), a grocery store, medical office, roads, traffic, sewers, restaurants, and retail, Bullock and team are basically building a branded, Margaritaville town. Bullock recognizes the challenge. "We have to meet customer expectations in three dimensions," he says. To help make the Latitude: Margaritaville vision a reality, he tells me the company hired a veteran of the Ritz-Carlton Hotel Company to join the team, to help develop customer-experience standards and protocols. It's just the beginning of a new way of speaking and catering to the older generation.

## KEY TAKEAWAYS

- Toss out old stereotypes about the over-fifty-five segment of the population. Being sixty-five or seventy years old doesn't mean the same thing it did even a generation ago. People are staying active, social, and youthful more than ever before—especially women. This is also the age group that has most of the money.
- There is a "coolness" and style gap for products and services targeted to this age group, especially for women.

## ACTIVATING YOUR INSIGHTS

- Determine how well you are engaging this group of potential customers. Is your approach in tune with the reality of their lives? What ways might you be able to promote opportunities for "reinvention" and experiences to this customer market?

- Baby boomer women are a loyal source of referrals for the people and businesses that serve them well. Be conscious of giving the same high standard of attentive service to all your customers, no matter what their age.

## TREND #6: PERSONALIZATION—"I AM MY OWN BRAND"

Funeral director Tasha Parker once had a fairly predictable job: she worked at a funeral home. Day in and day out, she helped families organize services that hadn't changed much in years: a casket viewing followed by a church service followed by a cemetery burial. People who wanted cremations received their loved one's ashes in an urn, held a memorial service, and drove home.

That was then.

Now, Parker works for Everest Funeral Concierge, the first funeral concierge service in North America. "Things are so different," says Parker. "People are putting their cremated remains on rockets. They're having memorial services in parks. They're making jewelry out of cremated remains. They're releasing balloons with cremated remains inside. Our motto is, as long as it's legal and achievable, we'll get it done for you."

As Parker's experience shows, we're living in the age of personalization, a societal shift I call "I am my own brand." Typically, we hear about personalization in the context of technology, e-commerce, and services like Netflix, but the desire for it goes far beyond that and into services of all kinds—even funerals. Looking at how one company achieves personalization in the funeral industry gives us a vivid example of how deeply it can drive emotional engagement in any business.

At this point you may be thinking, *Wait; back up. What's a funeral concierge service? Am I supposed to know?*

Everest created the funeral-concierge category: it's a Houston-based company that disrupted the funeral industry by providing independent, on-demand, personalized funeral planning. The company's services can be used with any funeral home in the world, and are typically included as part of a life-insurance plan: 25 million people in the United States and Canada have Everest as part of their life-insurance policies, either through their employer or through their individual policy. Everest filled a marketplace need for guidance on navigating what is often the third-largest expense in someone's life, behind the purchases of a home and an automobile.[17]

"You have six months to plan a wedding and you get six hours to plan a funeral," says Mark Duffey, Everest founder and CEO. "The process is opaque, and most people have little-to-no experience planning one. Jamming all that lack of information into a short, decision-making window is not acceptable for today's consumers, so we built a business model around becoming the consumers' independent advocate. The majority of our clients are women, so Everest was designed to meet their needs." This female focus was what first brought me to Everest, which I work with as a client of my firm.

Here's how it works. An Everest advisor works with a customer to determine what the family would like to do for their loved one. A traditional funeral? A cremation? A special event in a place that meant something to the deceased? Once a decision has been made, Everest will contact funeral homes on the customers' behalf and negotiate a competitive price. From there, Everest advisors work with the funeral home to coordinate all the service elements, including the creation of personalized materials such as obituaries, slideshows, videos, and playlists. If a customer wants skydivers and bagpipes or a catered lunch at a favorite restaurant with printed napkins and a commemorative drink, the advisor will coordinate those activities too. An important differentiator for Everest is that its insurance carrier partners dispatch a check to cover funeral costs within two days, instead of the more standard time frame of one month, which helps eliminate one enormous source of funeral stress: the money.

Many people are now forgoing traditional funerals and hosting celebrations of life that uniquely reflect the interests and passions of their loved ones. This is a sign of the times. People want to be able to design their own experiences, in life as well as in death. It's as true in B2B services as it is in the consumer marketplace, and it's especially true for women. We are still in the early stages of the personalization trend, and it's growing exponentially. How can your business be a part of it?

## KEY TAKEAWAYS

- Personalization drives emotional engagement. The ability to deliver it can disrupt industries, as Everest has done in the funeral business.
- Personalization has high consumer appeal, particularly for women, who are Everest's primary customers.

## ACTIVATING YOUR INSIGHTS

- Determine where personalized options could fit into your product or service portfolio, and the kinds of resources that would be required to bring these options to market.
- Examine whether it would be appropriate or feasible for your business to provide tiered levels of service or a concierge-style, on-demand offering.

Now that we've covered six of the biggest trends impacting women's purchasing decisions, you have all the pieces in place to create strategies that will be relevant to your customers and prospects. Let's recap them here:

1. Double Duty, Half the Time
2. The Mini-Me Effect
3. Visual Storytelling
4. Health and Wellness as a Lifestyle

5. Sixty Is the New Forty
6. Personalization—"I Am My Own Brand"

It's time to bring together everything we've covered to start planning and executing your new strategies for growing your business. We'll close out our time together with a Monday morning action plan.

## CHAPTER 9

# YOUR MONDAY MORNING ACTION PLAN

W e've covered a lot of territory in this book. You've learned dozens of ideas for using your own personality and strengths to *connect* with customers; *inspire* them to do business with you; instill *confidence*; and demonstrate *appreciation*. And you've generated your own ideas along the way. The Four Motivators Framework gives you a dynamic tool for growing your business by engaging women as customers. As you've seen, many of the strategies are broad enough to appeal to men, too, thereby providing an inclusive experience for all of your customers.

You've heard from leading brands, businesses, and sales leaders who are approaching the women's market opportunity in creative ways, from innovating new technologies, like Sephora, to revolutionizing business models, like Everest, to catering to modern families, like the PGA of America.

The six trends have provided context for how women are living and buying at this moment in our culture, to help ensure that your business practices are as relevant as they can be. Now the question is, where to begin? And for those of you who already have efforts well underway, where can you deepen your investments and expand?

I recommend the following action plan for bringing these efforts to life in your own business. Whether these steps serve as starting points or check-in points for you, knowing where your business stands provides a strong foundation from which to grow.

## ACTION 1: BENCHMARK AND SET GOALS.

In chapter 1, you ranked your business on a scale of 1 to 10 in terms of its effectiveness in connecting with women consumers. Use this number as a benchmark going forward. What would a "10" look like for you, and what actions would need to happen for you to get to that number? How long would it take? From there, determine the current gender split of your customer base. This number can serve as your second benchmark. Set specific goals: By following The Four Motivators Framework in this book, what kind of customer growth could you expect to see in one year? In five years? And what do these numbers mean in terms of potential revenue increases for your business?

## ACTION 2: GAIN A DEEPER UNDERSTANDING OF FEEDBACK FROM YOUR EXISTING CUSTOMERS.

What kind of feedback are you currently receiving from women customers? Does it differ from that of your male customers? If you have the analytics available, examine the gender split of customer feedback and look for service-enhancement opportunities. Can you tap into one or more of the six macro trends to take customer experiences to the next level? If you work with retail partners, ask for their help in providing information that will help you better understand how their customers view service experiences in these channels. When possible, collaborate with these partners to take customer experiences to the next level.

## ACTION 3: LISTEN TO WHAT CUSTOMERS ARE SAYING ON SOCIAL MEDIA.

If you represent a brand, people are talking about it on social media. As much as you can, leverage social listening tools to determine how women are talking about your business online. How engaged are they in your industry category? What brands do they mention most? What are they saying about your competitors? What do they love? What frustrates them? Visit relevant websites and social channels to uncover how women are talking about your business. Use these insights to inform your customer experience strategy.

## ACTION 4: IDENTIFY WHAT'S ALREADY WORKING WELL, AND DO MORE OF IT.

Your business is already successful at engaging women as customers at some level. Now that you have a new set of insights, you can better analyze why some aspects of your business may have more appeal with women consumers than others. What are the elements that are already working well? Once you've identified them, find ways to replicate or expand these initiatives. If you have team members that are successful in these areas, work with them to document and teach their best practices to the rest of your staff.

## ACTION 5: CONDUCT YOUR OWN RESEARCH.

Verify that your customer insights are up to date. Consumer journeys are changing fast. You probably have competitors today that didn't exist three years ago. Your customers have new expectations too. If your firm hasn't conducted market research with women in the last three years, it's time to get out in the field.

If you're a solo practitioner, there are many simple and inexpensive ways to conduct your own research. One is to schedule time to talk to your most important customers (and former customers) to hear their viewpoints on industry issues and the products and services they need most. These conversations might just give you new ideas for expanding your business. There are also many inexpensive survey tools available. Find a research method that works for you, and make it your goal to know your customers better than anyone else.

## ACTION 6: ASSESS YOUR CUSTOMER-
## FACING MATERIALS AND SPACES.

Armed with your new insights, assess your physical spaces as well as your marketing materials, signs, and website design. Do you have an inclusive representation of men and women, in both words (including pronoun use) and images? Are the photographs current, or do they feel outdated and stereotyped? If in doubt, get feedback on your current marketing materials from a representative group of women who will give you their candid opinions. From a physical space standpoint, determine which areas of your physical space are easiest to improve and which areas require a longer-term investment. If you could do only one thing to make your space more inviting for women, what would it be?

## ACTION 7: TRAIN YOUR TEAMS AND STRENGTHEN THEIR DIVERSITY.

If your business has a formal sales training program, be sure that it encompasses women's viewpoints as well as those of your male customers. Without an inclusive program, your colleagues are at risk of missing communication skills that will enable them to connect with this crucial market and, at worst, may alienate the very people they're trying to attract.

One idea for a fast start: consider creating a women's advisory board of customers and/or influencers, and solicit the group's input.

Strive for more diverse, gender-balanced teams both internally and externally, including with agency and vendor partners. Research shows that gender-balanced teams achieve greater results. McKinsey and Company has demonstrated that companies in the top quartile for gender diversity are 15 percent more likely to have financial returns above their respective national industry medians.[1]

As you've seen throughout this book, the absence of a female lens on business strategies is a blind spot that companies often discover too late—after they've failed to connect with their audience.

## ACTION 8: PILOT. REPEAT. PILOT. REPEAT.

There are dozens of ideas in this book—and those don't even include all the ones you've come up with while reading it. Some of them will be appropriate for your business, and some won't, but hopefully all of them got you thinking in a new direction. Armed with these fresh insights and The Four Motivators Framework, test new concepts, products, and ideas. And then repeat the process. Remember that short-term strategies are the enemy of success. If a maiden effort fails, try something else, because once is not enough. I've often heard executives say, "We tried to increase our numbers with women customers, but it didn't work." I would inevitably find out that they had tried one initiative, one time, and when it wasn't an immediate success, they never did anything again.

Repeat.

## ACTION 9: MEASURE.

With benchmarks (created in Action 1), it's much easier to measure the impact of new initiatives. Determine how many areas of the business you can benchmark, and begin the process for the current year. Strive to build on your success every year, and stay committed to fostering a more inclusive approach throughout your organization.

## ACTION 10: MAINTAIN YOUR RELEVANCE TO WOMEN CUSTOMERS OVER THE LONG TERM.

As our time together draws to a close, allow me to add one final and somewhat unusual suggestion for achieving long-term success: get out of your office or work environment, at least temporarily.

Many years ago, I worked for a great boss who told me something I've never forgotten. He came to our offices one day and found me working at my desk. His brows furrowed, and he said, "It always makes me sad to see you at your desk. I don't want to see you here. I want to see an empty chair and know that you are out in the field, talking to our clients and finding new ones. You won't find them behind that desk."[2] His words had an impact on me. I started to realize that the most successful people I knew were the ones who prioritized getting out of the office and spending time with their current customers and target customers. They visited retail partners and distributors. They shopped competitors. They held their own seminars. They made time to go to networking events, civic events, and conferences. They engaged in the world their customers lived in.

Who has time for that? You do. I do. We all do. Everyone, from presidents to professional athletes, has the same twenty-four hours in a day that we do. Engaging externally is one of the best ways to stay relevant with women, because their purchasing patterns—and female culture—are shifting all the time. Here are a couple of specific strategies for getting out and going to your customers:

## Engage in female culture.

Spend a morning or afternoon visiting brick-and-mortar retailers that are popular with women in your customer base. Notice the ways these stores communicate through language, visuals, merchandising, and customer service. What lessons can be learned?[3]

Business books are vital (please allow me to say thank you for buying this one), but don't stop your professional reading there. Check out the bestseller lists at least monthly to stay current on what women are reading, and make it a goal to read autobiographies by contemporary women authors. There are far too many fantastic authors to list here, but if you don't know where to start, try *Bossypants* by Tina Fey (New York: Little, Brown, 2011).

Subscribe to or follow the social media accounts of prominent women's publications. Not only will they give you insights on how women communicate with one another; they'll provide you with good examples of copywriting styles. You'll be surprised by how much you can learn about women's culture in the small pockets of time between attending meetings, catching airplanes, and waiting for conference calls to start.

Use a similar strategy to follow influential women on social networks.

Finally, turn your attention to TV and movies that feature female protagonists and plotlines. Get plugged in to the world of women's culture, and you'll be amazed at how much more relevant your ideas—and conversations—become.

## Take field trips.

What are the chances of having a bold, brilliant idea while you're hunched over your keyboard? Not as good as if you've been out and about first. Every week, build time into your schedule to get out in the field at least once. This can mean anything: visit a customer; hit some retail stores; go to a conference; say yes to someone who wants to have coffee with you; give a presentation to a class at a local university; see a new play. Getting fresh stimuli from new people and experiences will have a positive impact on your work. You will meet new customers. You will sharpen your skills as an observer. You will also be giving serendipity a chance to work its magic.[4]

Women's consumer domination is here for the long term. With The Four Motivators Framework and the strategies and tools presented in this book, you're ready to win her business.

# ACKNOWLEDGMENTS

Books grow the ways plants do. Each one starts as the seed of an idea, and in order for that idea to grow and bloom into an actual book, the author needs the right environment. The following people have created that environment for me and served as the sunshine, water, and fertile soil that made this book possible:

Erik Orelind, my extraordinary husband, who moved heaven and earth to support me in this endeavor and inspires me every day; Rosemarie Brennan, my mother and role model since I was old enough to crawl; Mary Ellen Smith; Joe Smith; Chloe Smith; Charlotte Smith; Katy Brennan; Genna Brennan; Caroline Brennan; Patricia Brennan; Bob Orelind; Greger Orelind; Susie Orelind; Alex Orelind; Emma Orelind; Sofia Orelind; Kajsa Orelind; Jackson Lamy; Niklas Lamy; Sylvia Decker; Tom Decker; Annie Decker; Alexander Decker; Rick Wilson; Rod Keith; Jared Champlin; Greg Brisson; Kevin Toukoumidis,

Leslie Ramirez; Jeff Bailey; Nina Szidon; Tom Szidon; Jason Batchko; Lisa Oldson; Heiko Dorenwendt; Anne Marie Carver; Katherine Teske; Susanna Homan; Michelle Sanchez; Grant Deady; Barby Siegel; Joe Versace; Karen Farquhar; Curt Wang; Joao Varandas; Laurel Bellows; Mark Partridge; Daniel Rogna; our valued Female Factor clients; my speaking clients around the world; all the executives who've graciously shared their stories in this book; and the great team at HarperCollins Leadership, including Jessica Wong, Amanda Bauch, Jeff James, Sicily Axton, and Hiram Centeno, and Brian Hampton.

# APPENDIX

Throughout the book, you've had the opportunity to apply your learning in each chapter's "Activating Your Insights" sections. For your convenience, all of those exercises are included here in the appendix. Enjoy!

## CHAPTER 1

### YOUR BIGGEST GROWTH MARKET IS ALREADY HERE

- If you were to rank your business on a scale of 1 to 10 on its effectiveness in connecting with modern women consumers, with 10 being the highest, what number would you give? Use this number as a benchmark for future progress.
- How have you seen differences in gender culture play out in your own customer interactions? What did you learn from these experiences?
- Categorize your customer data by gender. Can you identify specific buying patterns and preferences by examining the information this way?

## CHAPTER 2

### WHAT SELLING LOOKS LIKE NOW

- Think about the best buying experience you've ever had with a sales professional. What did that professional do well that made the experience so memorable? What lessons can you apply to your own business based on that experience?
- Write down your favorite places to shop/buy/be a

customer, including both e-commerce companies and traditional businesses. What are these companies doing well that you could adapt for your own business?

## CHAPTER 3

## THE FOUR MOTIVATORS FRAMEWORK

- Thinking about your own business and sales style, which motivators are your greatest strengths? Which need the most work?
  - My ability to connect
  - My ability to inspire
  - My ability to make customers feel confident
  - My proactivity in showing appreciation
- Imagine your customer is talking to a friend. Your customer tells her friend, "You *have* to work with [YOU], because ____ _____." What are the reasons you'd like the customer to give? How many can you come up with that don't involve price?
- Evaluate your business environment by seeing it through the lens of women customers. Answer the following questions, which reflect some of the things women may be noticing when they enter your place of business:
  - Does this place feel bright and modern?
  - Is the space clean?

- Did I get a friendly welcome when I walked in?
- Do the people here make me feel comfortable (i.e., are they polite and respectful)?
- Are there any women working here?
- Is there a place for me and/or my companions to sit down?
- Do they cater to people with kids?
- Do they show an interest in helping me?
- Do the people here seem knowledgeable and trustworthy?
- Do they offer good value for the price?
- Can I count on them if something goes wrong with my purchase?
- Would I want to come back here?
- Do I feel compelled to tell my friends they need to come here?

## CHAPTER 4

## MOTIVATOR #1: CONNECTED: CREATE AN EMOTIONAL CONNECTION WITH YOUR CUSTOMERS

- Imagine that someone felt so strongly connected to your business that she wanted to get a tattoo of your logo. (Work with me here—it's a brainstorm! And don't forget, people already do this with brands such as Harley-Davidson and Nike.) What are the kinds of things you could do to generate that kind of loyalty and connection? Create a list of ideas, and pick the top one or two to execute.

- What are the three top ways that you connect with customers currently? How can you expand on these efforts to create even deeper connections?

## CHAPTER 5

## MOTIVATOR #2: INSPIRED: INSPIRE YOUR CUSTOMERS TO DO BUSINESS WITH YOU

- Your best customer stories can inspire prospects and new customers. With that in mind, consider creating a "Happy Customer Story Repository." This repository is a compilation of your best and most inspiring customer stories, documented in a file so that they're top of mind and can be referenced in future customer conversations. If you work with a team, collaborate on the repository so you can share each other's customer stories and have that many more to tell.
- Think about all the things you do for customers that might cause them to say, "Wow!" What are some ways you can

create more "wow" moments, like the test showers at Kohler Experience Centers and the test rides at Folsom Bike? Can you expand on the "wow" moments you already offer?

- Ultimately, people are inspired to buy something when they feel it will improve their lives. How can you more effectively articulate how much better someone's life will be if they buy your product or service?

## CHAPTER 6

## MOTIVATOR #3: CONFIDENT: INSTILL CUSTOMERS' CONFIDENCE IN YOU AND YOUR PRODUCTS

- In what ways can you give your customers just 5 percent more than they're expecting (in terms of service), every time?
- Revisit your online professional profile. Is it up to date? Does it create a compelling impression of your capabilities? If you don't have a professional profile, make it a priority to create one.
- What analog activities in your own business could you bolster with technology, similar to the way Sephora uses technology to bolster customer confidence in its company and products?

## CHAPTER 7

## MOTIVATOR #4: APPRECIATED: MAKE YOUR CUSTOMERS FEEL APPRECIATED FOR THEIR BUSINESS

- What are some creative ways you can show appreciation to your customers? You don't have to break the bank. In my neighborhood, two nail salons are on the same street. One offers a free, two-minute shoulder massage with each manicure, and one doesn't. Guess which one gets my business?
- If you created a loyalty program for your business, what could it look like?
- Identify the obstacles that prevent you from keeping in regular touch with customers and influencers. What can you do to make this process more manageable?

## CHAPTER 8

## TOP TRENDS DRIVING WOMEN'S BUYING PATTERNS: A ROAD MAP TO EXCEEDING CUSTOMER EXPECTATIONS

### Trend #1: Double Duty, Half the Time

- Many of the apps that Judi uses provide a helpful service, not a product. Could you offer a complementary service for the products you sell? For example, IKEA bought TaskRabbit, an app-based business that helps people with errands and activities such as assembling IKEA furniture. It was a natural match. Ulta Beauty stores offer a variety of hair and beauty treatments. How else can you make your customers' lives easier with a service that complements your products? Can you leverage new technologies to offer conveniences such as deliveries and automatic replenishment?

- Time is only one aspect of convenience. Write a list of other aspects of convenience that you can provide through your business.

## Trend #2: The Mini-Me Effect

- Consider how this trend could be an opportunity for your business to grow. Does it make sense for your brand to move up or down the age spectrum? Is there an opportunity to provide "parallel programming" for both kids and parents?
- Pets are a part of the family too, and a fast-growing sector of the consumer economy. Determine whether your business has an opportunity here too.

## Trend #3: Visual Storytelling

- Brainstorm creative ways to inspire customers to include you, your products, or your services in their social media posts.
- How can you be a part of the new wave of mini milestones in our culture?

## Trend #4: Health and Wellness as a Lifestyle

- Identify the health and wellness trends influencing your customers right now. Are there any latent health and wellness qualities you can tap into within your own business?

- In what ways can you demonstrate that your product or service is "good for you"? Write down as many as possible.

## Trend #5: Sixty Is the New Forty

- Determine how well you are engaging this group of potential customers. Is your approach in tune with the reality of their lives? What ways might you be able to promote opportunities for "reinvention" and experiences to this customer market?

- Baby boomer women are a loyal source of referrals for the people and businesses that serve them well. Be conscious of giving the same high standard of attentive service to all your customers, no matter what their age.

## Trend #6: Personalization—"I Am My Own Brand"

- Determine where personalized options could fit into your product or service portfolio, and the kinds of resources that would be required to bring these options to market.

- Examine whether it would be appropriate or feasible for your business to provide tiered levels of service or a concierge-style, on-demand offering.

# ABOUT THE AUTHOR

Bridget Brennan is the CEO of Female Factor, the world's top consultancy focused on women consumers. She is the leading professional speaker on the subject of engaging women as customers and decision makers. She is also the author of the book *Why She Buys: The New Strategy for Reaching the World's Most Powerful Consumers* (Crown Business, 2011). In her work, she's conducted research with thousands of women on their purchasing habits and preferences, and provides counsel to *Fortune* 500 companies on developing strategies to grow their businesses. She was named a "Woman to Watch in Retail Disruption" by the Remodista social think tank and is a contributing writer for Forbes.com. Additionally, she is a member of the Vikings Women Advisory Board of the Minnesota Vikings National Football League team and a frequent guest lecturer at universities.

In her work at Female Factor, Brennan developed a sales training program that has been implemented successfully at major companies throughout the United States. Based in Chicago, she is a sought-after presenter at conferences and industry events around the world. Learn more about her at www.bridgetbrennan.com.

# NOTES

## Introduction

1. See, for example, Michael J. Silverstein and Kate Sayre, "The Female Economy," *Harvard Business Review*, September 2009, https://hbr.org/2009/09/the-female-economy, citing a 2009 Boston Consulting Group worldwide survey; Bridget Brennan, *Why She Buys: The New Strategy for Reaching the World's Most Powerful Consumers* (New York: Crown Business, 2011); United States Department of Labor, Employee Benefits Security Administration, "General Facts on Women and Job-Based Health" fact sheet, DOL.gov, December 2013, https://www.dol.gov/sites/default/files/ebsa/about-ebsa/our-activities/resource-center/fact-sheets/women-and-job-based-health.pdf.

2. The concept of gender as cross-cultural communication

was pioneered by linguistics scholar Deborah Tannen of Georgetown University, author of many insightful books on gender, including *You Just Don't Understand: Women and Men in Conversation* (William Morrow, 1990, 2007). The concept of applying gender culture in marketing was popularized by Marti Barletta, in her book *Marketing to Women: How to Increase Your Share of the World's Largest Market* (Dearborn Trade Publishing, 2006).

## Chapter 1

1. Silverstein and Sayre, "The Female Economy" (see intro., n. 1).
2. Bridget Brennan, "The Real Reason Women Shop More Than Men," Forbes.com, March 6, 2013, https://www.forbes.com /sites/bridgetbrennan/2013/03/06/the-real-reason-women -shop-more-than-men/#5dd4274f74b9.
3. United States Department of Labor, Bureau of Labor Statistics, "Volunteering in the United States, 2015," news release no. USDL-16–0363, February 25, 2016, https:// www.bls.gov/news.release/volun.nr0.htm.
4. United States Department of Labor, "General Facts on Women and Job-Based Health" (see intro., n. 1).
5. Brennan, *Why She Buys*, 179 (see intro., n. 1).
6. For an excellent overview of the topic and references to studies on the subject, see Rose Hackman, "'Women Are Just Better at This Stuff': Is Emotional Labor Feminism's Next Frontier?," *Guardian*, November 8, 2015, https:// www.theguardian.com/world/2015/nov/08/women -gender-roles-sexism-emotional-labor-feminism.

7. National Center for Education Statistics, Table 318.10. "Degrees Conferred by Postsecondary Institutions, by Level of Degree and Sex of Student: Selected Years, 1869–70 through 2026–27," *Digest of Education Statistics*, March 2017, https://nces.ed.gov/programs/digest/d16/tables/dt16_318.10.asp.

8. ICEF, "Women Are Increasingly Outpacing Men's Higher Education Participation in Many World Markets," October 22, 2014, http://monitor.icef.com/2014/10/women-increasingly-outpacing-mens-higher-education-participation-many-world-markets/.

9. Jeff Guo, "Women Are Dominating Men at College. Blame Sexism," *Washington Post*, December 11, 2014, https://www.washingtonpost.com/news/storyline/wp/2014/12/11/women-are-dominating-men-at-college-blame-sexism/?utm_term=.69d88c5e4b57.

10. United States Department of Labor, Women's Bureau Issue. Working Mothers Brief, June 2016, https://www.dol.gov/wb/resources/WB_WorkingMothers_508_FinalJune13.pdf.

11. United States Department of Labor, Women's Bureau.

12. United States Department of Labor, Women's Bureau.

13. United States Department of Labor, Women's Bureau.

14. BMO Wealth Institute, "Financial Concerns of Women," March 2015, https://www.bmo.com/privatebank/pdf/Q1–2015-Wealth-Institute-Report-Financial-Concerns-of-Women.pdf, p. 2.

15. See Robert W. Fairlie et al., *The Kauffman Index of Startup Activity, 2016* (Ewing Marion Kauffman Foundation, August 2016), available at www.kauffman.org/~/media/kauffman_org

/microsites/kauffman_index/startup_activity_2016
/kauffman_index_startup_activity_national_trends_2016.pdf.

16. American Express, "The 2017 State of Women-Owned
Business Report," http://about.americanexpress.com/news
/docs/2017-State-of-Women-Owned-Businesses-Report.pdf,
p. 3. Women-owned businesses are defined as those that are
at least 51 percent owned, operated, and controlled by one or
more women.

17. United States Department of Labor, Bureau of Labor
Statistics, BLS Report no. 1065, April 2017, https://www.bls
.gov/opub/reports/womens-databook/2016/home.htm.

18. Pew Research Center, "Social Media Fact Sheet," February 5,
2018, http://www.pewinternet.org/fact-sheet/social-media/.

19. Statista, "Percentage of Teenagers in the United
States Who Use Snapchat," Statista.com, March
2018, https://www.statista.com/statistics/419388/
us-teen-snapchat-users-gender-reach/.

20. Sandrine Devillard et al., "Women Matter 2016: Reinventing
the Workplace to Unlock the Potential of Gender Diversity,"
McKinsey Global Institute, https://www.mckinsey.com/~
/media/mckinsey/featured%20insights/women%20matter
/reinventing%20the%20workplace%20for%20greater%20
gender%20diversity/women-matter-2016-reinventing-the
-workplace-to-unlock-the-potential-of-gender-diversity.ashx,
p. 22.

21. Devillard et al., "Women Matter."

22. Catalyst, "Women CEOs of the S&P 500," October 5, 2018,
https://www.catalyst.org/knowledge/women-ceos-sp-500.

23. Valentina Zarya, "Female Founders Got 2% of Venture Capital Dollars in 2017," *Fortune*, January 31, 2018, http://fortune.com/2018/01/31/female-founders-venture-capital-2017/.

## Chapter 2

1. Accenture, "U.S. Companies Losing Customers as Consumers Demand More Human Interaction," March 23, 2016, https://newsroom.accenture.com/news/us-companies-losing -customers-as-consumers-demand-more-human-interaction -accenture-strategy-study-finds.htm.

## Chapter 3

1. Brennan, *Why She Buys*, 259 (see intro., n. 1).
2. Liz Hampton, "Women Comprise Nearly Half of NFL, but More Wanted," Reuters, February 4, 2017, https://www.reuters.com/article/us-nfl-superbowl-women/women -comprise-nearly-half-of-nfl-audience-but-more-wanted-idUSKBN15J0UY.
3. Minnesota Vikings staff, in discussion with the author, n.d.
4. Minnesota Vikings, "Vikings and MSFA to Open New Mothers' Room at U.S. Bank Stadium," press release, August 23, 2018, https://www.vikings.com/news/vikings-and-mfsa -to-open-new-mother-s-room-at-u-s-bank-stadium.
5. Steven Bertoni, "WeWork Hits $20 Billion Valuation in New Funding Round," Forbes.com, July 10, 2017, https://www.forbes.com/sites/stevenbertoni/2017/07/10 /wework-hits-20-billion-valuation-in-new-funding-round/.
6. Michael Brown, Andres Mendoza-Pena, and Mike Moriarty,

"On Solid Ground: Brick-and-Mortar Is the Foundation of
Omnichannel Retailing," AT Kearney, 2014, https://www
.atkearney.com/documents/20152/924670/On+Solid+Ground.
pdf/1958eca8-df9f-da6e-a02d-82f2039bbd63.
7. Ed Hammond and Noah Buhayar, "Buffett's Berkshire
Hathaway Buys Stake in Pilot Flying J," Bloomberg.com,
October 3, 2017, https://www.bloomberg.com/news/articles
/2017–10–03/buffett-s-berkshire-hathaway-acquires
-stake-in-pilot-flying-j.

## Chapter 4

1. United States Department of Labor, "General Facts on
Women and Job-Based Health" (see intro., n. 1).
2. Bridget Brennan, "Would You Like Champagne with That
Sofa? Restoration Hardware Bets Big on Experiential Retail,"
Forbes.com, November 13, 2015, https://www.forbes.com
/sites/bridgetbrennan/2015/11/13/would-you-like-champagne
-with-that-sofa-restoration-hardware-bets-big-on-experiential
-retail/#479af4bb1c60.
3. Brennan, *Why She Buys*, 260 (see intro., n. 1).
4. *Pretty Woman*, directed by Garry Marshall, Touchstone
Pictures, Silver Screen Partners IV, and Regency International
Pictures, 1990, film.

## Chapter 5

1. Brennan, *Why She Buys*, 238 (see intro., n. 1).
2. Bridget Brennan, "The Retailer Winning the Battle for
Millennial Women," Forbes.com, November 16, 2012, https://

www.forbes.com/sites/bridgetbrennan/2012/11/16
/the-retailer-winning-the-battle-for-millennial-women
/#35d780076ea9.

3. Adapted from Bridget Brennan, "We're All Millennials Now," Forbes.com, October 16, 2014, https://www.forbes.com /sites/bridgetbrennan/2014/10/16/were-all-millennials-now /#288c42e13241.

4. Brennan, "We're All Millennials Now."

5. See Bridget Brennan, "Three Strategies for Marketing to Millennial Women," Forbes.com, November 12, 2013, https://www.forbes.com/sites/bridgetbrennan/2013/11/12 /three-strategies-for-marketing-to-millennial-women/.

6. Adapted from Bridget Brennan, "Avoid These Visual Mistakes When Marketing to Women," Forbes.com, October 7, 2015, https://www.forbes.com/sites/bridgetbrennan/2015/10/07 /avoid-these-visual-mistakes-when-marketing-to-women /#4fff64cb5e50.

7. The US television sitcom set in a friendly bar, which ran from 1982–1993.

## Chapter 6

1. Laura M. Holson, "How Sephora Is Thriving amid a Retail Crisis," *New York Times*, May 11, 2017, https://www.nytimes. com/2017/05/11/fashion/sephora-beauty-retail-technology .html.

2. Brennan, *Why She Buys*, 245 (see intro., n. 1).

3. Frank V. Cespedes and Jared Hamilton, "Selling to Customers Who Do Their Homework Online," *Harvard Business Review*,

March 16, 2016, https://hbr.org/2016/03/selling-to-customers
-who-do-their-homework-online.

## Chapter 7

1. "About Allstate," Allstate Insurance Company, accessed
   September 23, 2018, https://www.allstate.com/about.aspx.
2. Data provided by MonteNapoleone District.
3. Adapted and updated from Bridget Brennan, "How to Deliver
   the Ultimate in Luxury Retail Experiences, Italian Style,"
   Forbes.com, July 12, 2016, https://www.forbes.com/sites
   /bridgetbrennan/2016/07/12/how-to-deliver-the-ultimate-in
   -luxury-retail-experiences-italian-style/#868b1946a894.

## Chapter 8

1. Ruth Schwartz Cowan, *More Work for Mother* (New York:
   Basic Books, 1983), 18.
2. Bridget Brennan, "The Growth of Women in the Workforce
   and How Retailers Can Respond," Forbes.com, February 28,
   2017, https://www.forbes.com/sites/bridgetbrennan/2017/02
   /28/the-growth-of-women-in-the-workforce-and-how
   -retailers-can-respond/#266f53524b1d.
3. Adapted from Bridget Brennan, "Why Parents and Kids Now
   Aspire to the Same Brands," Forbes.com, March 12, 2012,
   https://www.forbes.com/sites/bridgetbrennan/2012/03/12
   /why-kids-and-parents-now-aspire-to-the-same-brands
   /#77b30eb92bd6.
4. Brennan, "We're All Millennials Now" (see ch. 5, n. 4).
5. Interview excerpted from Bridget Brennan, "Parallel

Programming Attracts New Players," *PGA Magazine* and PGA of America *New Player Engagement Series* podcast, August 2016. Used with permission from the PGA of America.

6. Ronan J. O'Shea, "Luxury Hotel Provides 'Instagram Butlers' to Help Guests Take the Best Shots," *Independent*, October 18, 2017, https://www.independent.co.uk/travel/news-and-advice /instagram-butlers-photos-hotel-maldives-resort-conrad -hilton-best-guide-a8006656.html.

7. Check it out on Gugu Guru, at https://guguguru.com /dominos_registry.

8. Bridget Brennan, "A Picture Is Worth 1,000 Likes: How to Create an Engaging Customer Experience at Retail," Forbes. com, April 7, 2016, https://www.forbes.com/sites /bridgetbrennan/2016/04/07/a-picture-is-worth-1000 -likes-how-to-create-an-engaging-customer-experience-at -retail/#306554ff431d.

9. Adapted from Bridget Brennan, "From Farm to Label: The Wellness Trend in Marketing Goes Far Beyond Food," Forbes .com, November 12, 2014, https://www.forbes.com/sites /bridgetbrennan/2014/11/12/from-farm-to-label-the-wellness -trend-in-marketing-goes-far-beyond-food/#754ae02f2f56.

10. United States Department of Labor, "General Facts on Women and Job-Based Health" (see intro., n. 1).

11. Adapted from Bridget Brennan, "Marketing to Women? Age Is Really Just a Number," Forbes.com, June 14, 2016, https:// www.forbes.com/sites/bridgetbrennan/2016/06/14/marketing -to-women-age-is-really-just-a-number/#1387b6a978d9.

12. AARP and Oxford Economics, "The Longevity Economy:

How People over 50 Are Driving Economic and Social Value in the US," AARP.org, September 2016, https://www
.aarp.org/content/dam/aarp/home-and-family/personal
-technology/2016/09/2016-Longevity-Economy-AARP.pdf.

13. Shelagh Daly Miller, "Adults 50-Plus Now Dominate All Consumer Spending," *Ad Age*, November 18, 2015, based on data from the US Consumer Expenditure Survey, http://adage.com/article/aarp-media-sales/adults-50-dominate-consumer-spending/301391/.

14. AARP and Oxford Economics, "The Longevity Economy."

15. Adapted from Brennan, "Marketing to Women? Age Is Really Just a Number."

16. "Changes in Composition of New Entrepreneurs by Age," in Fairlie et al., *The Kauffman Index of Startup Activity, 2016*, fig. 5A (see chap. 1, n. 15). According to the author's calculations, 24.3 percent of new entrepreneurs are between the ages of fifty-five and sixty-four, compared to 25 percent for ages twenty to thirty-four.

17. Sandra B. Eskin, *Preneed Funeral and Burial Arrangements: A Summary of State Statutes* (AARP Public Policy Institute, 1999), https://assets.aarp.org/rgcenter/consume/d17093
_preneed.pdf.

## Chapter 9

1. Vivian Hunt, Dennis Layton, and Sara Prince, "Why Diversity Matters," McKinsey & Company website, January 2015, https://www.mckinsey.com/business-functions/organization
/our-insights/why-diversity-matters.

2. Adapted from Bridget Brennan, "Marketing to Women? Creative Inspiration Is Closer Than You Think," Forbes.com, April 28, 2017, https://www.forbes.com/sites /bridgetbrennan/2017/04/28/marketing-to-women-creative -inspiration-is-closer-than-you-think/#77ca93333622.

3. Brennan, "Marketing to Women."

4. Brennan, "Marketing to Women."